Don't Wait...

FOR THE WORLD TO GET BETTER

KATIE YOUNG

About The Author

When physical and mental illness took her to a crossroads in life, Katie turned her focus to healing herself and then working with others in client-based therapy. Her main qualifications are based in Nutrition, Reflexology, Reiki, Energy Healing, Flower Essence Therapy, Kinesiology, Anatomy and Physiology, Pathology for the Complementary Therapist, Iridology and she holds certificates in many natural food and nature based trainings. She has spent many years challenging herself to investigate beyond the conventional views regarding health, wellbeing, and human potential.

Katie has been a qualified therapist since 1997 and has worked with many inspirational clients. She has experience working in varied environments including Private Medical Practice, Health Clubs and Private Practice. Katie has also held posts on boards of Therapy Organisations and Teaches Accredited Complementary Therapy Courses and Workshops with her colleague and friend Elisabeth.

Katie is originally from London, England, and now lives in Kent with her husband, two children, two cats and two dogs. In no particular order, she loves good food, loves spending time with her family, loves her work, is in love with Ibiza and Minions (yes, the little yellow people ☺), feels most alive when in nature and special friends are very important to her. Katie is grateful every day, never stops learning and appreciates her most difficult times were her biggest blessings.

Dear Melissa,

So happy our paths have crossed x

Thank you for you!

Much love,

Katie

xxxx♡☺

ISBN: 978-1-9163512-1-9

Rev. date: 12th Sept 2022
Second Edition

This book is dedicated to everyone who has the courage to step up and be something other than what is expected of them.

Contents

How to get the best from this book

To ensure you get the best from this book, I invite you to read it from beginning to end in chapter order starting with the introduction (which is super important for the understanding of the whole book).

I have specifically designed this book to include some short 'Don't Wait Assignments'. This means, you hold in your hands a mix of a book, a meaningful discussion, and a course all rolled into one.

By including these assignments, you avoid continuous reading, and you can allow the information in chapters to resonate, flow, and sink into your being. You will be able to have fun with the information, better understand and retain what is most important to you and implement new discoveries into your life with more ease.

Follow each chapter in order, and *gift yourself with the time to complete* the mini assignments, there is no deadline, no time limit, but make it clear to yourself upfront that these are *non-negotiable*, they are there for a reason and will be super supportive and empowering. You can have assignments running alongside reading a new chapter or pause reading while you immerse yourself in the assignment, find what works best for you.

The Don't Wait Assignments are not designed to send you into super serious personal development, self-healing mode, that is just another way of ego distracting you from yourself. Remember you are already perfect, so there can be no healing to do… only healing of the mind, and the mind is just an inventor of stories. Keep it light, you are on a journey of magical discovery, don't judge anything, all will be revealed to you by You as we head along this journey together.

I would recommend dedicating a journal specifically to your journey with this book. You may already have a 'Don't Wait Journal' ☺ to record your thoughts and assignments, if not, visit www.divineroyalty.co.uk or use any beautiful journal that you have. Your written thoughts often hold the key to great guidance and opportunities, so fill your journal with anything and everything that pops up for you on this journey.

To accompany this experience, I have some products including Vibrational Essences and Essence Candles that are designed to beautifully support your personal experience of integrating new information and assisting you to connect with the divine part of yourself more easily. If you feel drawn to them, they can beautifully enhance your reading experience and life. The products can be found at www.divineroyalty.co.uk

Lastly yes there are some science bits in the early chapters, if like me you find the science stuff a bit challenging, I have kept it simple and I encourage you not to skip these bits. They help link everything together so your life experiences will make much more sense.

Introduction

Don't Wait a Second Longer…

It's more important than ever to take your destiny into your own hands.

Listed here are a few of the common side effects (of which I've experienced at least 99% of at some point) of living a life that has its focus outside of yourself, relying on the world to get better, so you can be better…

- Fear (very, very, few people live without some kind of fear)
- Anxiety
- Depression
- Worry
- Overactive mind (wow, can that chatter go on, and on…)
- Stress
- Pushing yourself too hard
- Striving towards goals at the expense of your wellbeing
- Having no goals
- Boredom
- Feeling sad
- Lack of energy
- Overwhelm
- Insecurities
- Feeling lost
- Feeling like you should be happy, but you aren't
- Lack of self confidence
- Lack of self-care and self-love
- Feeing out of control
- Feeling like something is missing, that there must be something more

If I'd written a self-description of my inner world 20 plus years ago that would have been me, right there, all that stuff whizzing round inside me.

If you can see yourself in 1, 2, 6 or all the above points you are not alone. I have worked in the field of health, personal and spiritual development as a mentor, coach, therapist, researcher, and tutor for over 25 years, and never have I seen so many of these emotions rising in people with such speed and momentum.

The thing is, when these feelings rise, there is a massive positive to be found in them… if they aren't left, aren't ignored, like I ignored them!

As I sat on the end of my bed, I'm not sure if it was morning, afternoon, or evening… everything became still, and I heard the words that changed my life forever.

I wasn't sure where the words were coming from, it was like someone else talking in my head. It wasn't the usual rambles on loop, this was a quiet, firm, and certain voice, and its message was very clear "it's time to step up or leave". It wasn't referring to leaving the room, we were talking leaving this world, my life, we were talking final choice point.

I now know that the voice I heard was me, it was that quiet voice that lives within us all, which is rarely heard due to the ongoing noise of the world, and the more dominating voice in your head. You will know the quiet voice I'm referring to when I say it's the voice that we sometimes call intuition, knowing, or a gut feeling.

I had been ignoring that voice within forever, only listening to the dominating bla bla bla in my head, the loud voice that dictates every decision and action we take, and every emotion we feel.

We all ignore that quiet voice of immense wisdom and guidance because we are often busy striving to possess those shiny things that show our success, striving to fill an empty space within that cannot be filled with stuff, or anything else in the world, but us.

Everyone has been affected by the world events that commenced in 2020, and the effects will continue to ripple through humanity for years to come. Handled in the right way, this can be the breakthrough you and humanity have been waiting for. This global situation provides the exact opportunity to connect with your Soul, the Divine part of you, that quiet voice within.

Let me tell you, not listening to that quiet voice can get you in a whole heap of trouble! It's exactly how I reached my step up or leave moment. I wasn't listening to ME I looked to the world, society, for all answers and guidance. In fact, I didn't know I had, or could have, any other reference point than what society and the world had to offer me.

I had known for a long time I was missing something, that there must be something more, but I didn't have a clue what that meant or what to do about it. As I sat on the end of my bed having ignored all the mental, emotional, and physical signs for so long, I knew my body was failing and it was just a matter of time before the final curtain came down on my life.

At my core I was always (as are you) a creative soul, but nothing in society supported that part of me, nothing in society validated that I could be anything other than 'normal' and fit into a box that society, and the people around me had designed for me, via their expectations of how I should fit into the world.

I navigated myself through early years adoption, bullying, lack of confidence, feeling stupid academically at school (because I didn't understand the system and why I was taught so much that wouldn't serve me in the world), insecurity, and socially shy.

I think being in the school system was the starting point for the foundation of me not believing in my own inbuilt wisdom, knowing, intuition, and feelings. I was to fit in, and anything that questioned otherwise was just me being silly.

This was further compounded as I moved through life, falling into jobs and situations that were not what I wanted or needed to make me feel alive, to light up that part of me that was trying to express itself in the world.

I did what society said, "do what others do, do what you should, what is expected, and don't think too much for yourself, these are your options, pick one".

From such a young age I moved through life compromising myself, not choosing the things that I felt my soul was trying to guide me to, I lost my unique spark of life and began to just disappear into the loop of robotic living. I closed the guidance of my soul, that creative, wise sat nav, that was guiding me to express my uniqueness in the world. I then forgot that the world needed my unique light, as it needs yours too.

Whether it be relationships, money, health, job, purpose, or just living life, if you are trying to fit into something without listening to the creative calling of your soul, life won't ever be smooth... on the outside maybe, but on the inside, you will tell a different story of unfulfillment and restriction.

This is how I moved through my life for so long, unfulfilled, and restricted, I was just not internally happy, on the outside I was doing fine, fitting in my box nicely, but inside I was slowly dying (literally).
In that end of the bed moment, I questioned myself... if I left this world now, what would be my legacy, what would my eulogy say?

I know if I had written it at that time with honesty, there would have been such gaps of unfulfilled possibilities to my life, and there would be such sadness running through the script because I hadn't lived my precious, precious life honouring myself and serving the world with my uniqueness.

That certainly bought things into perspective!

Some deep questions arose, and I realised many things about my life and how I still had so much to give, to share, to be, to experience, and that I had never expressed who I truly was, the whole me, the Katie that had her unique reason for being here, not the Katie that had been carved out or moulded to fit into what society expected. That all led to one question… when that final curtain comes down, will I smile knowing I lived life really, really well?

The answer to that question, at that point, was no. I had lived expressing myself as a version of others truth, as an expression of everyone who had influenced my life, I had not uncovered the possibilities, gifts, and joy that awaits us all, of living as my true self.

So, there I was in my step up or leave moment and I heard that voice again, it told me "It's not your time, you have more to do, but you have to stand in your power".

That was a relief!

I had no idea what stand in my power meant, let alone how to find out, but at the same time I somehow knew, on some level, if I made the decision to be me, I would be guided, and it would be the start of something quite important.

True enough, from that day onwards I was guided, little by little at first. I was learning to hear and act on a new type of guidance, from that day onwards the most incredible journey began.

I had to heal myself first, I figured if I could heal my physical the rest would follow. Sure enough, as promised, what I needed appeared including the opportunity, time, and funds to train as a Nutritional Consultant. Through my training I didn't only study and qualify, I healed my body in the process.

Having healed my physical body, the mental and emotional side of health then became an obsession to understand, not just for myself but also for others, I wanted the whole picture not just part of it.

Becoming healthy emotionally, physically, spiritually, and mentally by understanding who you actually are, not just your human labels, is more important than it has ever been for your personal happiness and fulfilment, and for the sake of the earth and the survival of all species, including us as a species.

So, as a much healthier me, I went on to qualify in a varied number of health, wellbeing, and natural therapies, including Spiritual Healing, Reiki, Energy Therapy, Reflexology, Kinesiology, Iridology, Anatomy and Physiology, Pathology, Energy Essence Therapy, and many natural food and nature-based trainings.

A bit further down the line I also qualified as a Tutor teaching others Accredited Therapy Courses, I held posts on boards of Therapy Organisation's, ran Workshops, Retreats, and worked one to one with clients in Private Practice in various settings, including Private Medical Practice, Sport and Fitness, and my own Private Practice.

Throughout all this study and experience, my biggest learning came from my personal journey of healing, personal and spiritual development, my questioning of every aspect of life, our existence and all my personal actions, reactions, and circumstances. The other greatest teacher for me was having the honour and privilege of sharing so many others personal life journeys and challenges through my work with clients.

What became strikingly apparent the more I worked with clients, and with my own personal development, was that there were no real answers to those big questions we all have, and why all our lives are touched by such an array of life circumstances and challenges. There were no real answers beyond the standard schooling, religious teachings, medical and scientific conclusions.

There was no information that addressed the bigger questions such as where do we come from, why are we here, what's our purpose while we are on earth, who are we apart from the name and physical identity we have, where are we going next, is this it, what are we humans truly capable of, and why have we personally, and globally got into such difficulties?

Why do most of us suffer from all, or at least some of the above points I mentioned earlier?

I couldn't find this information in a complete down to earth form; I couldn't find a book that linked all the information together and didn't just include parts of the jigsaw. So, I decided to write one!

That sent me on a mission that I now know is my reason for being here… my purpose is to uncover the answers to the big questions we all have and share them with you.

When I realised that, when I felt it in my heart, I made a declaration to myself, and the universe, that I would find these answers, because I wanted to stop people reaching the point I did, and I wanted to help others live the life they dream of, the magical life we are all designed in human form to live.

It is my purpose to help you know that you don't have to wait for the world to get better, because there is an incredible story that you have forgotten, that holds the key to everything… this story is your history, our history it is what joins us together as one, and knowing it determines whether you can say at the final curtain… I lived life really, really, well!

After making that declaration, I have spent the past 25 years on a mission to push the boundaries set by society, modern science and medicine, regarding human potential, human existence, and our place in the universe. I have investigated and learnt through personal experience that all those feelings I listed earlier are NOT who you are, they are coping mechanisms that have been put in place because of the amnesia of who you truly are.

I have walked the walk through these discoveries, to be honest at times I have screamed, cried, and crawled through the learning to uncover what lies beneath the human us. The reason things got so tricky for me was, after making that declaration, I thought things would be all flowers and answers dropping into my lap (hilarious conclusion), but what I didn't realise was that to uncover what was under all the layers of human stuff, such as emotions, learned behaviour, trauma, inherited beliefs, societal programming etc I personally had to remove these layers in me, to uncover what lay underneath them.

For me to shift that lot, it meant that my life was going to get very challenging, because it was the challenges that bought up ALL the emotions that were keeping me from really seeing and hearing the wisdom that was within me, who I was under the human me, and what our true story and place in the universe was.

So, in came the challenges and life circumstances that triggered every lower emotion you could imagine anger, fear, deep hurt, neglect, pain, trauma, feeling scared, lost, terrified, sadness, out of control, bitterness, overwhelm, mental and physical burn out, and being pushed to my limits consistently.

To give you a little peep into my learnings, some of my challenges included losing my dear dad in terribly traumatic circumstances due to other people's errors, this was my greatest learning to release the emotions of anger, resentment, and blame, and it was my biggest teacher of forgiveness.

My wonderful mum's 13 years of horrific mental illness and being her sole carer with 2 children under 3 opened a vast array of challenges for myself and my family. I was manipulated, controlled, threatened, and the list of emotions it bought up was almost limitless... but they were brought up for me to see past them, look deep inside me and as I released these emotions there was a space left for me to connect with something far deeper, a deeper wisdom that would be my guide in and through these times.

The reason I not only got through all my challenges, but also came out of them thriving, happy, and fulfilled is because in that end of the bed moment when I heard myself, I learnt the most important part to living a magical life, no matter what is going on around you, and that is to listen to the other part of yourself, the divine you.

As I accumulated all the information I am going to share with you, I learnt that without doubt I have a place within me that is unshakable, and that knows that this human emotional rollercoaster ride we have created is absolutely not who we are. When you know who you actually are, the struggle loses its grip, the fear dissolves, life becomes lighter, peaceful, abundant, and you stop searching for something outside of yourself.

Over the years I have come to know, without doubt, there is a massive chunk we have been missing about who we are, our place in the universe and the complete human story. This missing information has led to an amnesia of who we truly are, and amnesia leads to/is responsible for ALL the feelings that are listed in the above points, all personal and global challenges, and what we see reflected as our world.

If you woke tomorrow with complete amnesia to who you are, where you come from, why you are here and the purpose of your life, how would you feel?

Think about that for a moment now, how would you feel?

I think you would agree you would feel scared, uncertain, look for guidance outside yourself because you wouldn't know who you really are, you'd feel lost, out of control, overwhelmed, have lack of identity and therefore lack of self-love, anxiety, overwhelm, a need to control your circumstances, insecurity, a feeling there is something you are missing, the feeling you should be happy but you're not, and the biggest one of all...fear.

This my friend is exactly how we have been living for generations of time, we have forgotten our story, our history, and the truth of who we are, we have created a world based on the amnesia of our place in the universe, our greatness, and our eternal selves, we have based our lives on just being human... when the truth is, we are both human and divine combined.

At this time in human history, this truth about you is more relevant and urgent to rediscover than ever before.

There are signs everywhere that people are searching for answers through spiritual, energy, mindset mastery, health, nutrition, fitness, personal manifestation and personal development books, workshops, courses etc. All areas of personal and spiritual development are growing exponentially.

While I am completely supportive of all the self-education modalities, and think they are of huge value, when people embark on this personal improvement path one thing tends to happen and can continue to happen for all their lives... they end up in a loop of personal development learning.

You could start with mastering mindset, then move to self-empowerment, then manifestation, and you could go on for months and years, often flitting between one and another, and despite all of this, you still have unanswered questions, you still have insecurities, still have some of those feelings we talked about earlier, and it is a constant effort to maintain being in the space you have just learnt about.

Do you know why this is?

Do you know why despite all our efforts of personal development, questioning, and trying to get to that place where life just flows, that place of peace, certainty, abundance, happiness, self-love, and a life of real meaning, we never quite fully reach it?

Because my friend, we are missing a huge chunk of the most important part to elevating your life to the place you want it to be, we are missing the divine history we all share, the full story of ourselves, not just our human bit.

We have witnessed in quite difficult ways personally and globally where our human-only mindset has got us, and now it is time to have a new more complete story.

Without the understanding of your true design as human and divine combined, the loop of striving for that something will continue forever, because you will not be building your learning on a solid foundation of unwavering knowledge of your completeness.

Trying to live in happiness, and abundance without this solid foundation of knowledge is like building a house without solid foundations, you will be forever underpinning it with more bricks, things will crumble, and things will never be stable.

If however, you move forward with the solid foundation of your true history, where you come from, who you really are, why you are here,

and the incredibly powerful divine being that you are… nothing can shake you, everything you learn and place on top of that unshakable foundation will absolutely take you to where you want to go.
Your amnesia will be cured, and while there will be some work to do to create the life you want, and the world we want to share together… when you know your whole story you will never be without direction, support, unwavering strength, identity, certainty, abundance, and peace. If you embrace the information in this book with an open heart and mind, the list of feelings at the beginning of this introduction will not be something you identify yourself with any longer.

Instead, your list can look much more like this, I know because this is now my list too:

- Certainty
- Calm
- Clarity
- Love (of self, of life)
- Love (divine universal supportive, deep, and unwavering)
- Happiness
- Mindfulness (instead of worry)
- Relaxation
- Trust
- Knowing
- Inspired
- Excitement
- Wonder
- Wisdom
- Appreciation
- Gratitude
- Inner happiness
- Outer happiness
- Fun
- Abundance
- Thankful

- Reflective
- Awe
- A graceful understanding of life and death
- An ability to know that whatever is going on in the world you can glide through life and create your reality based on your reason for being here

My friend, it is time to find out who you are and to live the miraculous life you were designed to as human and divine combined, and with that comes the abundance, richness, and happiness that this life was always meant to hold for you.

Don't wait for the world to get better to make things better for you, that will never happen, because it's all within you, intertwined in the long, magnificent history you have beyond just this human you... when you live as human and divine combined, that is when life truly lights up!

In this book we are going on a journey together in which I will remind you of who you are, why you forgot, your place in the universe and how to live without restraint or restriction and transform that 'list' of feelings into happiness, freedom, expansion, abundance, and you will be able to smile at the end of each day knowing you are living life well.

Don't wait for the world to get better.

Much Love,

Katie

Chapter 1

Pushing The Boundaries

Throughout this book, when it comes to new perspectives and fresh ways of thinking, we will be doing a lot of boundary pushing, and this early stage of the book is no exception.

So, with that in mind, I want to start as we mean to go on and share some really important, life changing information about you, with you. We will expand on these facts and help satisfy your logical mind throughout the book, but for now, focus and read on with an open heart and an open mind.

The points below offer some very important information about you, (insert your name here).

1. There exists a creative conscious intelligence that created everything.

2. *Everything on our planet, YOU included, came from and are, consequently, that very same conscious creative intelligence.*

3. *YOU therefore, have within you the intelligence and wisdom of that which created everything.*

4. *You are not a victim of life you are the orchestrator of your life.*

5. ***YOUR body is not just the physical matter you 'see', you are made up of an incredible structure that's composition is eternal.***

6. ***YOU are empowered with infinite possibilities; you have the potential to access every answer to every life question you ever have.***

7. ***Within YOU there is a place where there is no fear, no struggle, no lack, because you know who you are and where you come from.***

8. ***YOU already know the theory of everything; you just need a few pointers to start remembering.***

You will probably never have been told this, been brought up to believe it, but it is the most honest truth ever!

If I had read the above points a few years back, I would have thought, "That's a bit deep. Lovely words, but they are only relevant to special people, holy people, people who make a big difference in this world. They are not words that in any way describe me, an ordinary girl, living an ordinary life." I don't even know if the words would have registered on any level at all.

The words would not have registered because, like most of us I was living my life, having the same general aspirations as everyone else, conforming to the guidelines that have been set by society and I guess living somewhat like a robot.

I worked in a job that was not my passion and worked all week to pay the bills. I would be told when and how much time I could have off work as holiday, I would live for the weekends and at the start of Monday be focused on Friday.

I would pay my bills, enjoy some alcohol and cigarettes, in varying quantities, to temporarily change my experience of life and chat with friends and family about everything I have just mentioned.

I, like many, for years based my life on the approval of others, and acquiring stuff to gain my identity, until I realised there was a real chance I could lose the most amazing opportunity, the most precious gift.

That precious gift of 'time'. Time between the miracle of birth, and the miracle of death. That very, very short time called 'Life'.

I too have been sucked in by the shiny things that we strive to possess to show our success. I have been distracted from myself, my life and its possibilities, by others drama and by creating my own drama to distract myself from myself. I too found my identity through sources external to myself.

I did not want to face those deeper questions that went beyond the identity I had carved out for myself. In fact, I didn't even know I didn't want to face those bigger questions, because I filled my life with everything your daily life gets filled with.

But that felt safe, I felt comfortable not delving into anything deeper. If I did, I'm sure there was laundry that needed to be loaded in the machine!

So, you see those '*important points*' and their meaning, could not be about me, I was just an average person.

One day, it all changed.

I had been unwell physically and mentally for some time. I was told I would need medication for the rest of my life, and I knew my body was falling apart.

I remember clearly to this day, sitting on the end of my bed, thinking at that moment "I need to do something, or I will not be on this earth for much longer". It was not a dramatic moment, but a calm clear thought process. At that moment I knew I had to take back my power, find some way to start healing my physical body, then fix the mental and emotional issues and the rest would follow.

From that point, I began living.

There is some interesting information coming your way, and I promise, you will connect with much of it on some level.

You see, those '*important points*' describe you and every person on this planet. But they are not who you identify yourself with. Your identity has become so detached from your origins. Your identity has become what you fill your life with.

My mission is to help reawaken within you the recognition of your pure beauty, complete perfection and your power as a creative being.

To help you realise, with sound information that the world we have created (full of fear, temporary satisfactions and materialistic aims) is certainly not the way it has to be.

The truth is, at some point, we will all have to face our departure from this world and then we will question our origins and where we are going next.

We will also question how we have lived our life. Have you loved enough, played enough, touched the sky with your gaze, and gasped at the beauty of the stars? Have you been in awe of our world and universe, have you honoured yourself, and loved yourself?

Have you touched people's lives, was your work your passion, have you left a positive imprint on the world, and ultimately haveyou 'really' lived?

Our eventual departure from this world is the most definite fact ever.

Before you depart, you can make sure you are living the best life and being the best version of you. Because YOU have everything you need within you to create your most incredible life.

I believe with every ounce of my being, that with the right information and support, combined with your openness and desire to know more, YOU will achieve amazing things.

The information to empower yourself and the world, is not just available to a chosen few. The knowledge of your origins, and your true wisdom is within YOU NOW.

You just need an explanation as to how you forgot, and some pointers to remember what is already there.

Do take advantage of everything I have found within myself and through the privilege of sharing others' life experiences. I offer this information freely to you and with an open heart.

Bring into your life and your heart what feels right for you and with my blessing use everything you can to create your best life and the best version of you possible.

Start finding the answers to those important questions now, so when your time comes to leave this earth and return Home, you will know you have lived the best life ever and your passing will be as natural as awakening to the sunrise.

So, at this point I invite you to be a part of the experience this book has to offer, its opportunities to embrace your potential, and have an incredible life through YOUR own empowerment.

Chapter 2

A Few Pointers

Before you embark on this book, become very aware of the voice in your head and the whisper in your heart.

We all hear it, every day rambling on in our heads, especially when we want to relax and shut down for a while.

Have you noticed how you can be watching TV or reading a book and if questioned about the content, you have no real idea what the story is about.

You have drifted off hand in hand with that voice while it rambles on about all sorts. It's very efficient at distracting you from yourself. It has had a huge amount of practice.

We live life guided by the voice in our head. The voice that likes to keep things the same, keep you in the same place, experiencing life through repetitive reactions. Reactions to various outside sources, and pre-programmed behaviour, going way, way back.

We will discuss these reactions in more detail later, but be aware that for the time being, for the majority of the time you have not actually been the one making the decisions that matter in your life.

Be vigilant! The voice in your head, aka your Ego, has all sorts of mad conclusions to base its commentary on.

This commentary keeps you living your life making the same decisions, having the same reactions, and continuously plays its commentary on repeat. The Ego voice will be one of your greatest obstacles when transforming yourself. Ego is a fear-based personality we have invented to survive in a world where we feel out of control. Ego stepped up to 'fully parent' us in the absence of our true guidance which it was never designed for. Ego is designed to look for threat and danger everywhere and in everything, and its programming is fear, lack, insecurity, and what if's.

So be aware of the hissy fits that may arise as you read this book and the Ego voice in your head tries to tighten the grip. You may hear your Ego as dismissive thoughts, confusion, elation and then disappointment, disbelief, irritability, fear, you're not good enough, sadness, anger, and the list goes on.

Alternatively, your Ego voice could be completely silent, and get you to drift off and ignore what you have read, pretending it never happened!

So, when you hear your Ego voice kick in (and you will), remember, you are already ahead of the game.

It's time to turn up the volume on your ***Intuition,*** turn the volume down on your Ego and brush its fear-based voice off your shoulder.

When you engage with your intuition, all sorts of amazing things can happen because the Ego voice in your head is no longer in charge.

Intuition; part of your inbuilt conscious intelligence

By harnessing your intuitions tremendous wisdom, you will bring your life to life.

It is so important to have some conscious awareness in place as you read this book. Awareness of how you are feeling and reacting during the experience of digesting the words.

I have placed such emphasis on this because, we spend a massive part of our life being directed and distracted by outside opinions that are not our own. We base most of our life decisions on those outside influences.

I am fully supportive of sharing and getting advice and guidance when needed. But no one can know you better than you. Whether it be your health, emotions, money, work, or relationships…you know you, it's just you have forgotten how to use and recognise honest self-talk and have given your inner knowing and power away to others.

I feel there is a real urgency to address ourselves, our lives, and the way we live. But this must be done in a state of awareness. Awareness of your thoughts, and in some cases harnessing raw courage, to face the fact that much of what you have based your life on, your beliefs and values, do not support you and are no longer relevant.

When you are fully supporting your own identity, it means you are not allowing yourself to be solely directed by the outside environment. To fully support your own identity and live from your intuition can be tricky at first.

This book is about you becoming empowered and reconnected to your 'quiet voice' called Intuition. Your Intuition talks to you more as a feeling, a wise, firm, balanced, and supportive feeling. A feeling that also has an air of quiet strength.

Do not get too hung up on the descriptive words and whether you have the right voice, or the right feeling. We have all experienced that gut feeling, an inner knowing about something.
The key words here are a feeling, to feel. You have to listen to your Intuitive voice but also feel it. You may be questioning, "what is this Intuition?" or "I'm not good at that Intuition thing" or "only gifted people have Intuition" (that will be the Ego voice chipping in).

In my experience ***everyone*** has intuition, an inner guidance, wisdom, an unbelievable knowledge they can draw on.

To gain further understanding of intuition, one dictionary describes it is as follows

Intuition is the ability to understand something instinctively, without the need for conscious reasoning. A thing that one knows, or considers likely, from instinctive FEELING, rather than conscious reasoning.

Common synonyms are: - a hunch, feeling, feeling in my bones, inkling, sneaking suspicion, impression, premonition and gut feeling.

All of us have had one of these intuitive feelings at some point. An inner knowing, a feeling about someone, a situation, a place, a job, a new home etc.

You are Intuitive!

The reason I have placed such emphasis on the importance of your Intuition, is because I want you to read this book not only using your intellect but ***with your Intuition fully engaged***.

That means paying attention to what you are feeling throughout.

As you read on, you will come across words, sentences, paragraphs and subjects that will resonate with you. You will feel something connect; you may fully understand why or may have no idea why.

These are the really exciting bits, when you feel something connect. You know on a level much deeper than your intellect, that you need to

understand more about whatever has resonated with you. You need to find out why you are signalling to yourself that this is relevant to you!

When this type of connection happens it is priceless, this has not come from someone else's viewpoint; this is **YOU** talking to **YOU**.

So, when something in this book feels right and resonates with you, acknowledge the prompt of your Intuition and your wisdom. Follow it up with some self-questioning, ask yourself why you feel connected, how does it make you feel, why is it relevant to you?

Investigate, because whatever it is, it will be a clue! It is a clue to an area of your life that needs more attention, more balance, and some transformational change. It may be that it is a clue to your passion, your direction in life. It may be a clue to what connects you to the real world, a world that is more relevant to you.

What I am saying is, if you 'feel' it, there is unquestionably a reason and with honest questions and honest self-talk, you will absolutely grow from your Intuitive prompts.

If you are prepared to be open and to listen consciously, your Intuition will guide you towards all that you want, all that you need and all that you can be.

Don't Wait Assignment

You have this book in your hands *because you are ready.* Ready to embrace something far greater than the restrictions the world has modelled for you so far, and this assignment is a great tool for you to have at the start of this journey.

As we have just spoken about in this chapter, the part of your mind that has been programmed to fear, to distract, and to keep you where you are, is the exact same part that may be freaked out by change and your desire to reclaim your life.

This is normal, you aren't self-sabotaging, you haven't got the wrong mindset, this is all part of the process of going from just human, with all the fear and restrictions, to the freedom and abundance of human and divine combined.

So, when this voice in your head pops up with all the reasons why you can't become the amazing version of you that you are designed to be, repeat this simple short sentence whenever needed, however many times it is needed, and in any situation… to bring you back to your truth point.

"May my Mind Thoughts be Replaced by my Divine thoughts"

This is a perfect and powerful statement for 3 reasons; firstly to tell your human ego that you are now in charge, secondly it informs the universe of your intention for the energy of your divine self to reconnect to your human aspect, and lastly you are confirming you are ready to be led by your own vast wisdom.

Write this down in your journal to use as a reminder, you can use post it notes around your house and workspace and repeat whenever your thoughts go off on an unhelpful tangent.

Chapter 3

Lost In A World Of Distractions

Identity and Significance

Before we can grasp a greater understanding of who we are, we need to review where we are personally at this time and where humanity is as a whole.

This is incredibly important because when we review humanity as a whole and realise we have come to accept the destruction of the earth, the extinction of many species and the habitual damaging of our health as normal, we must question how we have come to this point.

On a more personal level, many of us are physically unhealthy or suffering mental health issues. Stress is a massive part of our lives, low self-confidence and lack of self-love is commonplace, and when fear is often our strongest life motivator, we must ask ourselves questions.

We need to understand what motivates us to allow ourselves to be numb and accepting of this unbalance that is playing out all around us.

When we recognise what we have created as ourselves and why, we can then start the process of uncovering the real you and me. The real you and me who have gratitude and respect for this place we get to call home, and the real you and me who have such peace and solid self-love within, we no longer need to ignore all that we know is not right, and no longer need to accept life as something that just happens to us.

As humans, we are not thriving in every area, because we have taken ourselves too far away from our true nature, our origins and our natural way of being.

Everything on this planet thrives when it is allowed to be who or what it was originally meant to be. Everything thrives when allowed to express itself in line with its natural surroundings and through its inbuilt intelligence.

We like to think of ourselves as the most significant beings on this planet. What we have actually created in mankind is the most insignificant beings on this planet. Through detachment from our true nature, we have created an environment that encourages our insignificance.

We are pushing ourselves to thrive in a false environment. Pushing ourselves towards unnatural goals that will never fulfil us.

By creating this false environment, we have lost our place, our role, our understanding of our true nature and our connection to everything...we have lost our identity and significance.

Nature is something that holds its identity and significance in place beautifully, as naturally as the day it was created. Why?

Because it knows its place, its role on earth, it doesn't try to be anything other than its incredible self.

Living in a world of distractions we have lost our significance and identity and on our mission to find them, in all the wrong places, we mistreat ourselves, others and our planet. We are no longer connected to the knowledge and information that once ensured we knew who we were.

So now we look outside ourselves to find it. But it's not there, and that spells trouble, because in a race to find ourselves, we have become highly emotionally complex beings.

Since we became so disconnected from ourselves, our search for identity and significance is ultimately what drives us throughout our lives.

This dominating drive has not always been the motivation behind all we do. There was a time when we were absolutely connected to, and understood our origins. We had full awareness of our abilities as creators and stood in our power, with grace.

We had a connection with our human existence and our origins, in balance. We did not live with this one-sided human based existence that we now accept.

It goes back to those 'important points' we shared earlier. Our entire planet comes from and therefore is, the same awe-inspiring intelligence that created everything. You and me, we are that same creative intelligence, and you simply won't get any more significant than that!

This drive for identity and significance was absolutely not how it was or needs to be. This obsessive need for identity is something that we have developed within ourselves, in order to try and survive and feel relevant, in the false world we have created.

Most people's drive, actions and thought processes usually come down to the same things. An individual need to be **significant, loved**, and possess an **identity**. Because of course, we have misplaced our identity within our human experience.

Our imbalance and disconnection have created a need for all of us to strive for an identity within the realms of the material world, when in fact we will never, ever find it there.

Sure, we will have short-lived pleasure, whether it be via a new job title, a purchase, an event, but eventually we will need more, the said pleasure will become part of everyday life. We become bored with our purchases, possessions and titles; these external identities we build for ourselves will never be enough.

However, when you can go through life with a secure foundation and understanding of who you really are, you become centered, grounded, and secure within, you have nothing to prove. Our actions are no longer fuelled by the emotional complexities we have acquired in order to find ourselves.

When we lose the solely human drive, that is based purely on satisfying our emotional needs (Ego), we replace it with a balanced understanding of our humanity, our connection to everything and our power to create our own reality. We then become fully aware of our extraordinary significance. As a result, there is no longer anything to prove outside of our self!

We are here to enjoy life on this planet. We are most definitely not here to practice self-sacrifice to achieve greatness, ***we are already that greatness.***

With a clear connection to ourselves, we would never need to disrespect others, the earth, or ourselves. We would know we already have it all. We are creators and carry inside us that same divine intelligence that created us.

You are a creator and although you may be buried under a few layers of inherited and learnt stuff, there has never been so much available to help the authentic you to rise to the surface.

So, let's move forward and begin to understand what is beyond our obsession with this human based material existence.

Don't Wait Assignment

It's time to bring in, and give thanks for, the Divine You.

Use the following as a prayer/statement every day to help you absorb the empowering information in this book, re affirm your power and grace as a creator, and to offer gratitude for the guidance you receive every day.

Dear Universe,

I thank you for reminding me of my power as a divine creator, and that I have everything inside of me to create the divine, limitless life I desire, filled with happiness, joy, abundance, deep meaning, purpose, and love. ***I am*** *a Divine Creator, and from this moment on I claim my true status as Human and Divine combined.*

And so it is.

Chapter 4

A New And Very Important View Of You

Why we believe we are just our human suits...

We have become so accustomed to our belief in a purely human based existence; we now only view ourselves as our physical bodies, and little outside of that.

We commonly regard the universe and everything in it, as external to ourselves. And this is where a huge misunderstanding has occurred.

Over time we have created our insignificance and as a result, have had to develop a method of re-creating our significance.

The method? That voice in your head, your Ego. The voice that needs to be heard at all times, whose commentary is based on fear and insecurity, is supposedly right at all times and in control at all times, whatever the cost!

Our created insignificance brings with it uncertainty and instability. So we created the Ego self to cope and give us back our significance.

Our Ego keeps us in place with many emotional reactions, including insecurities, low self-confidence, greed, competitiveness, materialism, consumerism, and fear.

The Ego self has firmly imprinted itself within you, and over time it has tightened its grip and now all we believe in is our human characteristics and physical form.

Society reinforces your Ego beliefs, via the Ego beliefs of others, such as family, friends, and those who have influence in our society.

Through media, science, medicine, education, consumerism, and the government, our Ego's are bolstered and reinforced at almost every moment of the day, because pretty much ***everyone is operating from the same point of motivation and belief…Ego.***

This is not a judgement or criticism, Ego is simply the survival mechanism we now operate from, and completely believe we need.

So, anything outside of the current belief systems of social influence that could offer another view, will be met immediately with resistance. The Ego voice in your head, that is always 'right', will do whatever it takes to convince you 'this is the way it has always been and the only way'.

Not an easy thing to break free from when most others around you are operating from the same Ego belief system.

It is often during trauma or life crisis when a glimmer of something else appears within us, a much deeper 'us' that finds its voice, because we are forced into a space where all material things (Ego) and drama (Ego) no longer hold importance.

Due to our Ego selves, we have come to solely rely on our physical senses to interpret ourselves, and our world. Yet we are so much more.

The Ego self has you believe there is nothing other than you, nothing other than what you see, because if you could comprehend more than your physical traits, the Ego would no longer have control. The Ego would no longer have control because you would realise you are far greater than just your physical form, you would regain your significance and the ego would no longer serve a purpose and as a consequence lose its grip.

So how much more are we?

When my physical body was struggling to function, I took my health into my own hands and went back into education to study and qualify as a Nutritional Consultant. At that time it made sense to me that my physical body needed support and healing. A combination of using food and nutrition seemed the logical way to start putting myself back together.

At the same time I studied two different versions of Anatomy and Physiology, which gave me, for the first time, an understanding of how utterly incredible our physical bodies are. I also covered Pathology for the Complementary Therapist, and various other nutrition and physical health studies.

I did put myself back together physically and went on to work with others using my nutrition and health training.

Despite having good results, the more I worked with clients the more questions I had relating to what really helps us thrive.

The nutrition side of things was great, but I felt in pretty much all cases I was just treating symptoms. All be it with essential natural resources, I still wanted to know why people's bodies went wrong in the first place.

- Why do some have masses of energy and others do not?
- Why do some have mental health problems and others do not?
- Why do some have niggling health issues and others do not?
- Why do some have destructive behaviour patterns and others do not?
- Why do some have serious chronic illness and others do not?
- Why do some have major stress and others do not?
- Why do some survive illness and others do not? The more clients I worked with, the more I realised, there must be a big chunk of something I was missing.

Was health and wellbeing just the luck of the draw? Do we have any control over our health and life?

In pursuit of answers, I decided to expand my learning to include philosophies and practices that are not considered conventional, yet are practices that have been around successfully for ***thousands of years***, way before modern science and medicine. I figured if these practices had held their own for this long I needed to take a look.

I went on to study many different therapies, to give you some examples they included: Flower Essence Therapy, Kinesiology, Reflexology, Spiritual Healing, Reiki, Nature and Wild Foods, Iridology, and Energy Healing.

I challenged myself to push the boundaries set by modern day science and medicine regarding the theories of human form, human existence, and human potential.

Having studied and qualified in these therapies I went on to work extensively in the field of Client-based therapy, and eventually teaching too. Alongside, I continued to work hard on my own personal development and potential.

There was one common thread that seemed to underpin and link everything together. I had read about it and heard it bandied about in certain areas of health and wellbeing, but now I had first-hand experience of this golden key. It goes by many different names and ultimately, is the ***basis of everything***.

For me, it opened up a whole new understanding of human health and potential and is the open door to a fresh (but not new) view to understanding ourselves, the world, and the universe.

It has been known about for centuries, but when mentioned in conventional and in some cases alternative health circles, it can be met with anything from resistance to hostility.

By sharing this information with you I am not here to try and prove anything to you or defend my conclusions.

I share the facts of my personal experience working with these methods and the incredible changes I have witnessed in people's lives, including mine.

I have learnt everything from the ground up, been given no instruction book and no hi-tech equipment. I will not tell you how it is, I am here to share and offer information that has been gained by walking the walk. And I respect you and your intuitive intelligence to incorporate into your life only what feels right for you.

I am witnessing firsthand, that generally, people are more physically and mentally unhealthy than ever before.

Niggling, chronic and serious illness is rife, and people's lives are less fulfilled than ever.

Our world is under great strain and our planet is being trampled and abused.

It is urgently time to realise we need to be open to ***other options****, because our current way of living and caring for our world, and our selves is not working.*

The other options

The reason, I think, the subject I am about to cover, has been shied away from is because it was previously very difficult to prove scientifically. However, certain areas of science have now confirmed what I have personally experienced, and what ancient cultures have known about forever.

However, I also think this information challenges so much in our conventional world, that maybe it is simpler, or more convenient for some to continue to ignore it.

I cannot shy away from it, because unless we start to grasp the ***utter magnitude of its relevance to the existence of everything, and where this understanding can take us***, we will never fully move forward either in health, human understanding or in understanding the bigger picture of ourselves and the universe.

It's very nice having scientists and others who hold influence in our society working it all out for us, and sharing what they feel is appropriate, but you need to know this information too; this is your universe, your world, and your life.

How can we ignore something that has been experienced, acknowledged, and recorded for centuries?

I have studied and read many books relating to health, wellness, personal development and spirituality. But none of them gave me a solid, down to earth, easy to understand explanation, an explanation that links everything together. This one does.

Understanding bits of who you are will not get you to where you need to be, you will only ever get part way.

I don't want you to only have part of the picture; I want to pass on every last drop of learning and experience I can, to enable you to become empowered by your understanding of the whole.

So, as always, only take what feels right for you and **do** take notice of anything that creates even the smallest spark of interest within you.

This is how much more you are!

In eastern systems it is known as Life Force or Chi and in Quantum Physics it is referred to as Vibrational Energy.

It is the foundation of ancient science and the foundation of ancient medical systems. It is the basis of many ancient life practices.

And monumentally, this ***very same ancient knowledge*** of Vibrational Energy, as the foundation and practice upon which all life, health and understanding was based, is now the basis of some of the latest scientific research and discoveries, regarding ourselves, and the universe. This

Vibrating Life Force holds the key to everything.

Touching on science may or may not be your thing, but it is initially part of feeding and satisfying your 'logical' mind, and then expanding on this information using your own intuitive, experiential science!

The background of how we came to think in the way we do and draw opinions and conclusions about ourselves, and the universe, has come about by the information we have been given throughout our life. Not generally encouraged to question our education, we then accept (understandably) this information as truth.

How much you know about scientific theory is not important, but for now I will cover the relevant bits in order for you to have the basic information you need, to understand more about yourself, and the universe.

I understand that for some (like me), reading the science bit can be challenging, but I do encourage you to give it a go, it's a few pages over a couple of chapters and really does for the foundation to link everything together.

As we begin, it is appropriate to note and bear in mind, that Werner Heisenburg (Nobel prize winning Physicist and Philosopher) said:

"The problems of language are really serious. We want to speak about the structure of atoms, but we should remember that speaking about atoms in ordinary language is impossible". [2]

Here goes anyway!

[2] Werner Heisenberg – German Theoretical Physicist. Born 5th December 1901, Died 1st February 1976. Won the Nobel Prize for Physics in 1932.

Marvellous mathematics and, the end of trusting ourselves

Born on Christmas Day 1642, Isaac Newton was a British Physicist and Mathematician who contributed significantly to the 'scientific revolution'.[1]

In 1687 'Mathematical Principles of Natural Philosophy' was published, commonly known as 'Principia' and was acknowledged as the 'grand synthesis' of a ***mechanistic*** view that profoundly affected the path of mathematics, physics, astronomy, biology (including human biology), and chemistry.[1]

Newton's biggest contribution was the belief that all of nature and the universe could be explained by mathematics, and this was the driving force for what is known as the scientific method. Newton is best known for his discovery of the laws of motion, laws of universal gravitation and calculus.[1]

Although Newton's discoveries were fascinating, more important is the effect these discoveries had on how different branches of science developed.[1]

It is at this pivotal point in history that the foundation of modern medicines belief in the body as a measurable machine was solidified.[1]

Science then believed that all reality could be explained mathematically.[1]

Absolute knowledge could be pursued through mathematical calculation and ***without the 'weight' of philosophy, experience or the need to study***

[1] Bonny Casel, Quantum Botanicals Course, The Institute of Quantum Botanicals.

nature, human beings, or anything else in its natural circumstances and environment.[1]

Newton's discoveries meant that, whether observing the human body or the natural world, observation of the ***whole*** was replaced with ***methodical study of 'parts' of the whole, with no regard for the interaction between body systems, and the fact that matter is constantly changing and constantly affected by its environment.***[1]

This approach meant treatment of the *individual* by medical science was eliminated and instead medical science treated illness with a predetermined protocol. Using this method Nature is also regarded as mechanistic and measurable. The scientific method works on *statistical probability*, not individual experience.[1]

Science therefore, became a discipline that was independent from personal experience and personal knowledge and solely dependent on mathematical calculations and also heavily influenced by the 'experimenters' expectations.[1]

At this point knowledge that came from personal observation and experience became regarded as false and labelled as anecdotal (not necessarily true or reliable because it is based on personal accounts rather than 'facts' or 'research').[1]

Traditional medicine, based upon thousands of years of observation and experience was discredited. Knowledge gained from direct experience, was replaced by knowledge and evidence gained through experimentation (in unnatural surroundings), and qualified and quantified by mathematics.[1]

---

[1] Bonny Casel, Quantum Botanicals Course, The Institute of Quantum Botanicals.

Reducing us and the natural world to mathematics, birthed the scientific method.[1]

Truth became defined by scientific experimentation that produced repeatable results, without taking into account the whole. A scientific experiment focuses on an action and reaction within a very limited sphere that is predefined by the experimenter.[1]

But the universe is constantly changing. No two moments are ever the same. The human body is constantly changing, on all measurable scales.[1]

No two bodies, no two living organisms are the same. The scientific method cannot be applied without rounding off reality; therefore the results of the scientific method are always an estimation.[1]

Nobel prize winning German Physicist and Philosopher Werner Heisenburg said:

"We have to remember that what we observe is not nature herself, but nature exposed to our method of questioning".[2]

Mathematics is a powerful tool to communicate concepts when applied to areas such as mechanical engineering and theoretical physics, but it is a percentage game when applied to living organisms. Matter is in constant interaction with, and altered by, everything that it comes into contact with. ***Environment is everything, and this cannot be replicated in a laboratory.***[1]

[1] Bonny Casel, Quantum Botanicals Course, The Institute of Quantum Botanicals.

[2] Werner Heisenberg – German Theoretical Physicist. Born 5th December 1901, Died 1st February 1976. Won the Nobel Prize for Physics in 1932.

What is very interesting is that Newton's mechanistic view of nature, us and the universe, was overturned by physicists at the beginning of the 20th Century, and a new understanding of the nature of matter has solidified through irrefutable experimentation. Yet in certain areas of science, such as medical science, Newton's method seems to be an unshakeable view, which is fixed and no longer open to enquiry, despite science having moved on.[1]

In short Newton's discoveries led to the belief that all of nature could be understood mathematically, and birthed the idea of a clockwork, measurable and uniform universe.[1]

What is important to understand is the scientific method has remained sacrosanct within the natural sciences for 300 years, while knowledge of the nature of reality has evolved enormously over the last 100 years.[1]

Towards the end of his life Newton himself was dissatisfied with the application of algebra in the sciences, but by this time his discoveries had taken on a life of their own.[1]

The scientific method used in modern medicine hasn't changed to take into account what we now know about matter, the nature of consciousness, the relationship between the two, and the individual nature and interconnectedness of everything. However, outside the established medical community, science has some incredible new information to share.[1]

---

[1] Bonny Casel, Quantum Botanicals Course, The Institute of Quantum Botanicals.

So, now let's look at the new stuff

Born in Germany in 1858, Max Planck had a great interest in learning about the fundamental laws of physics and he began his studies at the University of Munich in 1874.[1]

Two hundred years after the Scientific method and Newton's discoveries, Max Planck was able to show that the energy of light (light, creates all matter) was proportional to its vibrational frequency, leading to the discovery of Planck Length (smallest known vibrational frequency) and Planck Mass (smallest known mass), which were able to define reality on a phenomenally small scale; the sub-atomic substance of matter.[1]

This showed that the laws of classical mechanics breaks down in the atomic world; the 'stuff' that we are made of is ***held together*** and ***formed by vibration*** and, if you look deep enough, there is no 'matter' at all, ***only vibrational energy.*** This discovery was the foundation for a new branch of science, called quantum physics.[1]

In 1944, nearing the end of his life, Max Planck said, "As a man who has devoted his whole life to the most clear headed science, to the study of matter, I can tell you as a result of my research about atoms this much":[3]

"There is no matter as such. All matter originates and exists only by virtue of a force, which brings the particle of an atom to vibration and holds this most minute solar system of the atom together.

---

[1] Bonny Casel, Quantum Botanicals Course, The Institute of Quantum Botanicals.

[3] Max Planck – German Physicist. Born 23rd April 1858, died 4th October 1947. Won the Nobel Prize for Physics in 1918.

We must assume behind this force the existence of a conscious and intelligent mind. This is the matrix of all matter." [3]

From Max Plancks perspective, all matter is formed by the coming together of vibrating particles, but behind the forming of these particles is intelligence, and consciousness, a conscious directed instruction.[1]

Max Planck was awarded the Nobel Prize in 1918 for his contribution to a new branch of physics, and is recognized as the father of quantum mechanics. Max Planck had a strong and influential friendship with the most famous scientist of all time Albert Einstein. Twenty years Einstein's senior Max Planck was one of the most respected scientists of his time.[1]

Albert Einstein was born in Germany in 1879 and was blessed with a family background that inspired his interest in science. He began his secondary education in Germany, and was a free thinker from the start, rebelling against the educational systems memorisation approach to study. Even so, he excelled in physics and mathematics.[1]

Einstein went on to complete a teaching degree in physics and mathematics, but had difficulty finding a teaching job. This didn't deter him from pursuing his exploration of mathematics, theoretical physics, and the philosophy of science. Einstein achieved his first post as a lecturer at the University of Bern.[1]

---

[1] Bonny Casel, Quantum Botanicals Course, The Institute of Quantum Botanicals.

[3] Max Planck – German Physicist. Born 23rd April 1858, died 4th October 1947. Won the Nobel Prize for Physics in 1918.

In 1905, Albert Einstein's *Annus Mirabillis* papers were published and reviewed by Max Planck, the then editor-in-chief of *Annalen der Physik (one of the oldest scientific journals),* and its co-editor, Wilhelm Wien.[1]

The Annus Mirabillis papers contained four works that, combined, contribute substantially to the foundation of modern physics and changed views on space, time and matter. The publication of Annus Mirabillis established Einstein as a top scientist and initiated a cascade of important discoveries, and in a very short period of time, the understanding of matter and the physical Universe had completely changed.[1]

Einstein and Planck's combined discoveries show that, if you look really deeply into the smallest known particle of matter, ***there is no matter; only vibrating energy.***[1]

Further research into sub-atomic and sub-sub-atomic particles has shown that the percentage of space in an atom is 99.9999999999999%.[1]

More recent advances that look further into this tiny percentage of matter in an atom, find that within even this small amount of matter is 'space', and this is one space, is the same space shared with every other atom across all space-time. In other words, you and I are not only made of vibrational energy, we are vibrationally 'one' and this 'one' not only manifests as you and I, it manifests as plants, stars, planets, nature, and space itself.[1]

On a quantum level of subatomic particles, all matter is frozen light; a type of energy pattern.[1]

---

[1] Bonny Casel, Quantum Botanicals Course, The Institute of Quantum Botanicals.

It took a while for science to progress to this understanding, but the foundation for this understanding came from the discoveries of Planck and Einstein:[1]

Frequency of vibration is what creates the illusion of matter.

All presentations of matter have their own vibrational frequency.

For example, the book or device you are holding has its own vibrational frequency, a tree has its own frequency, the air has a particular frequency, and you have your own frequency of vibration.

Whatever the frequency of vibration determines how the atoms come together to form matter.[1]

The Einstein viewpoint sees the body as a multi-dimensional organism made up of physical/cellular systems in dynamic interplay with complex regulatory energetic fields.[1]

Einstein showed that everything in the universe including human beings is comprised of this very same vibrational energy, i.e., the same energy from the same source.[1]

Quantum Theory tells us that ***everything*** is made up of subatomic (tiny) vibrating particles of energy.[1]

- These tiny particles that make up EVERYTHING in our physical world and the wider universe, are constantly moving, vibrating in waves and interacting with each other.[1]

---

[1] Bonny Casel, Quantum Botanicals Course, The Institute of Quantum Botanicals.

- YOU and I are included in this scientific conclusion, we are made up of these tiny vibrating particles of light, you and I are a mass of tiny particles of vibrating energy.[1]

- The speed at which these tiny particles vibrate determine how our physical senses interpret this energy, either as a solid, touchable object such as the device or book you are holding or as something out 'there' but unseen, like radio waves.[1]

- This vibrating energy that makes up you and everything in the universe, is known to be deathless, it cannot be destroyed, it only changes form.[1]

So, from this perspective,

- If you are made up of tiny particles of energy, that have no death, and only change form; how can you be just this human body?

- What are we before we have a physical body, and what are we after our physical body ceases to function/exist?

The answer...

- ***We are Vibrational Energy Beings. This mass of Life Force Energy is who we truly are. We are first and foremost VIBRATIONAL ENERGY that has a force/intelligence within it called consciousness.***[1]

As Quantum Theory states we are made from a mass of constantly moving, changing particles. We are not just a solid form; we are not just this human suit we temporarily wear.

[1] Bonny Casel, Quantum Botanicals Course, The Institute of Quantum Botanicals.

In no way do I want to undermine the importance of the scientific facts behind us as energy beings, however for those of you who are very visual, by looking at YouTube videos of the old Star Trek episodes, the 'energise' scenes give a good visual demonstration of us as tiny vibrating particles, constantly moving and changing form.

They show a human shape made up of millions of tiny vibrating particles.

Our human bodies are the ***ENERGY aspect of us that vibrates at the precise frequency to enable us to exist and thrive on earth.***

Don't Wait Assignment

This chapter presents the science behind who we are, and how we forgot the most powerful and magnificent part of ourselves. It may be a very new perspective for you, and as it is so important, your assignment is to go over the chapter and re read anything in **bold** and the **bullet points**.

As you re read, write down what this new understanding about you, about us, presents for you. How does it make you feel knowing that you are not just your human suit with its struggles and worries, but a powerful eternal conscious being, and part of an eternal universe?

[1] Bonny Casel, Quantum Botanicals Course, The Institute of Quantum Botanicals.

Chapter 5

Why We Believe Our Human World Is All There Is

The stumbling block we come up against in understanding and processing this scientific information, is we have been taught that what we see around us is all there is, and even more importantly everything we see around us is 'outside' ourselves, our world is 'out there', we look down at our body and see we are part of that 'out' there.[1]

So, lets look at how we came to the conclusion that everything is 'out there', and how we can understand a much, much wider view of our reality.[1]

Over the past few hundred years we have relied on the five senses of sight, hearing, smell, touch, and taste to communicate to our brain the aspects of the material world we live in, and our life experiences. This has been reinforced by the scientific method that has been developed to prove or disprove theories based on mathematical observation of the material world.[1]

---

[1] Bonny Casel, Quantum Botanicals Course, The Institute of Quantum Botanicals.

Although these five senses provide us with valuable information, much of it vital to our survival, these five senses can only provide information for about 0.0000000000001% of what is happening around and within ourselves.[1]

What is really crucial to recognise is our experience of life is not about the fact that the grass is green or the pen is black, the flowers smell fragrant or the birds are singing. ***These experiences add texture to life, but it is our inner life, our feelings, our thoughts, our consciousness, and how this interacts with our outer life, that makes up the majority of our experiences.***[1]

Our five senses tell us a great deal when encountering experiences in life but our ***'inner environment'*** communicates much more and defines how we experience our world 'out there'.[1]

From our earliest moments of consciousness in a physical body, we begin to learn about our world through our five senses, and we learn a language that is used to categorize and communicate these observations to our mind, and to others. We see and hear, taste, feel and smell, and these observations about the world around us define our physical world.[1]

So, how do we define our physical world, using our five senses as being 'out there'?[1]

All of the information that we receive about our outer world through our five senses is collected by our sense receptors. These sense receptors then convert the information into electrical impulses, which are transmitted by neurons (neurons carry messages through an electrochemical process) that are then decoded in the brain.[1]

---

1 Bonny Casel, Quantum Botanicals Course, The Institute of Quantum Botanicals.

The eye converts light frequencies and also converts a sense of spatial awareness, of distance and depth. The ears convert sound frequencies, the nose and tongue convert chemical frequencies, and the skin converts temperature, pressure and chemical frequencies. If we look at this in a little more detail through the sense of sight, as so much of the information about our world is based on sight.[1]

Photons are a fundamental particle of light. When we see an object, light clusters called photons travel from the object to the eye lens, where retinal ganglion cells turn the information received by light into electrical signals, which are transmitted by neurons to the centre of vision at the back of the brain.[1]

In this area of the brain information is received as electrical signals and decoded into images that we 'see' at this centre of the brain**. *The act of seeing doesn't happen 'out there', it happens in this area of the brain.***[1]

Science has shown us that the entire world we see, feel, smell, taste, and hear is ***vibration***, decoded by the brain. In fact, all that we think we are experiencing 'out there' is actually experienced inside of the brain.[1]

Considerable research now points to the possibility that the body we see and the brain itself that is seemingly decoding all of this information is no more 'out there' than the rest of the information that we decode.[1]

We look down at our body; our eyes convert the vibrational frequencies of light reflected back to us into electrical impulses, that the brain decodes as our body 'out there'. But does a physical body actually exist? Scientists

---

[1] Bonny Casel, Quantum Botanicals Course, The Institute of Quantum Botanicals.

have determined that, if it exists at all, then it only exists as vibration, i.e., as vibrating energy.[1]

Research suggests that it is very possible that everything that we identify as being 'out there', including the entire universe, our world, and our own bodies, doesn't exist. It doesn't exist, other than as an information energy matrix that ***our consciousness*** decodes as the three-dimensional world that we live in, there is no 'out there'.[1]

This is a big leap for our understanding of the universe from a scientific perspective. This theory, called Quantum Holographic Theory, or Holographic Universe Theory, has been put forward by leading quantum and string theory physicists, and are the primary scientific theories that explain much of what is known about our observable universe.[1]

Don't Wait Assignment

This is a mind and heart opening chapter, so I invite you to just allow this information to settle in and go back to any part of it that sparked your interest, or any part that you would like further time to absorb. Take notes, reflect and explore.

1 Bonny Casel, Quantum Botanicals Course, The Institute of Quantum Botanicals.

Chapter 6

How You Bring The World You See And Experience Into Form

Having now reached an understanding that everything in the universe is made up of tiny vibrating particles, that take their instruction from you as to what form they take, raises other questions.

The next question most people have is this. "If everything is made of tiny vibrating particles that are decoded in the brain to form pictures/images that we see as our world, do we all decode in the same way and do we all see the same things?"

A perfect question. This is another totally crucial part of the jigsaw towards understanding who you are and how you have the potential to transform and create your life! It is incredibly important.

You may have heard many quotes about the 'law of attraction', 'how you can create your life', and why 'positive thinking' is so important, well this is how and why.

There is a famous scientific experiment called the Double Slit Experiment, which shows the theory behind the fact that everything is made of vibrating particles and that ***we are responsible for their manifestation into form***.

The scientific experiment shows that all vibrating particles are actually vibrating particles of ***POTENTIAL*** and ***are awaiting OUR instruction to form matter.*** These particles are just potential, until we focus our attention on them, only then do they ***conform to our expectation*** to form matter.

This is why recognition and transformation of our programmed beliefs is so very important.

Our beliefs, and therefore our expectations are exactly what form our reality, that's it. No fate, no luck, no chance. The vibrating energy that makes up our world comes into form when we project our expectations on it. What you expect the world to look like, due to your conscious or learnt beliefs in the world, will manifest into form.

There is a great short video that will bring further clarity to your understanding of energy, potential, and the creator part you play in forming your reality. This famous experiment I referred to earlier is The Double Slit Experiment, initially conceived by Thomas Young (1773-1829). This particular video also touches on the concept of consciousness creation.

This version is from the film and book called 'What the Bleep'. Captain Quantum demonstrates the "most beautiful experiment of all time" as voted by readers of Physics World. You can find a short video by searching "Captain Double Slit Experiment' on your browser.

After watching this video I am sure you now have a really good grasp on the personal creation concept and wider universal connection we all share.

So now back to the question, do we all see the same things? Yes and no, here is why.

Everything in our world has its own energy information blueprint that has the potential to form an image/object.

Now remember at this point, nothing is manifested ***until*** we put our focus on it. When you put your focused ***expectations*** on it, ***only*** then does it become manifest.

It is an individual creation process that is guided either by your programmed beliefs or by your personal conscious creation to form your world.

Everything in this world is energy potential until we manifest it into form. This includes emotions, health, relationships, finances, and friends, every one of our experiences.

You can take this expectation and manifestation process and apply it to every area of your life.

Positive thinking can transform negative programmed behaviour into positive expectations. This is why the power of positive thinking works.
We have transformed our expectations (that all have their own energy vibration) from negative outcomes, to positive outcomes, this instructs energy that is still potential, to manifest according to our new expectations.

Spontaneous healing can occur because there has been a shift in understanding, expectations, and/or beliefs that our body is fully capable of healing itself and will heal. We believe our body is healthy, and therefore the potential of healthy cells are manifested by our expectations.

Processes of healing and transforming our lives can be simple and straightforward, but also situations and expectations can be multi-layered affairs (not resulting from just one incident), so changing the most obvious belief system doesn't always get immediate results.

Often we have to do a multi-layered transformation of our programmed beliefs to change what our expectations manifest.

I hope you can see the ***huge*** potential of these discoveries.

The world has a blueprint of many, many possibilities and it is you and only you that can activate the energy of these blueprints to form your world. ***Your beliefs and therefore your expectations instruct the vibrational energy of the world to form matter, to form everything in your life.***

As you now know our whole universe is comprised of vibrating particles of energy, everything we need to create the most magical life and world is here right now, all around you, little vibrating particles of potential.

The world is not a scary, unpredictable place. Our world holds the ***blueprint of perfection; it is only our beliefs and expectations, created by our emotional complexities that now create the world we experience.***

So, no, I don't think we all 'see' and experience the same things because at this point, everyone's expectations are different. Your individual beliefs and therefore expectations of the world are programmed by generations of others behaviour and teachings, influenced by society's collective beliefs and are continually being reinforced or challenged by your personal life experiences.

The planet's blueprint of potential is the same. How we interpret it, what we choose to 'see', manifest, and experience is individual.

The world at this moment is a reflection of how we feel about ourselves. It is a mirror of our Ego, feelings of insignificance, and need for identity. The world is a manifestation of our collective beliefs as a human race.

When you hear the saying "be the change you want to see in the world" you now know how this works and that it absolutely starts with each one of us taking responsibility for our thoughts, actions, emotions, behaviour, and beliefs. Because we all have a hand in building the world we live in through what we choose to manifest.

Every person whose thoughts and behaviour can be free of fear and Ego will change their personal energy vibration, this will create a ripple effect across the world, because as you know, we all share the same space!

How we 'see' and experience the world is up to us, every moment, every day.

Let's have a quick summary of how our human experience and the planet that supports that experience works.

- Everything on earth is made of vibrating particles of ***potential.***
- Everything that makes up our planet and our human selves (including thoughts and emotions) starts off as an energetic blueprint of potential, ***awaiting our instruction.***
- Each one of us in human form is physically equipped to manifest these blueprints into feelings, emotions, form, and experiences.
- How we 'see' and create our experiences in life is based purely on our expectations. ***Particles of potential react to our expectations to form what we believe or expect we will see and experience.***

With a world of energy potential, just awaiting our instruction, you can see where free will comes in. We have the world of potential at our fingertips, we are physically equipped with everything we need to manifest, and have free will to choose what we manifest.

This is how the 'law of attraction', 'positive thinking', 'prayer', 'affirmations', and other such processes actually work.

Each one is an energy manifestation, good or bad in our lives, they are all energy manifestations, via your thoughts, beliefs and expectations. These personal manifestations form your world and your life experience.

What we see and experience as real is a projection of our own unconscious, programmed, Ego beliefs **or** our authentic conscious instruction. Your expectations are the instructions, creating the illusion of a material world, via the manifestation of vibrational energy forming 'matter'.

You create the material world via conscious thought and emotion, which then instructs the vibrating energy particles to form your 'reality' according to your beliefs and expectations. You are the creator of your reality.

How incredibly exciting and ***empowering*** is that bit of information? ***You*** have the inbuilt capacity to create.

Don't Wait Assignment

This chapter is probably one of THE most important things you will ever read when it comes to understanding You, the world, and how to create the life you desire. It is the most empowering information available to us, and when understood and embraced has the potential to create anything you desire in your life, and for us to return to living in a world of reverence and respect for the whole.

It removes the need for competitiveness, dependence on the world to get better before we can get better, and fear, because we know that we have within us the power to create our own reality and freedom to live as we desire.

For this assignment I invite you to reflect on 2 situations in your life and do the following:

Situation 1 – take a situation in your life that isn't working too well, something that is challenging you on some level, relationship, financial, work anything that is unbalanced.

Next focus on the situation, what and who is involved, the emotions that are bought up for you, how it makes you feel.

I would like you to *feel* the reactions rather than going straight to the mind for 'judgment'.

Then ask your Divine guidance "Is this a Mind or Divine situation"?

Sit with this for a while and see what arises from the question and write down your thoughts.

No pressure this is pure contemplation time for you.

Situation 2 – now take a situation that is working well in your life, something that is balanced, makes you happy, and makes your life experience better.

Focus on this situation, who and what is involved, the emotions it brings up for you, how it makes you feel. I would like you to *feel* the reactions rather than going straight to the mind for 'judgment'.

Then ask your Divine guidance "Is this a Mind or Divine situation"?

Sit with this for a while and see what arises from the question and write down your thoughts in your journal.

When you have completed both exercises, compare your thoughts, feelings, and what you wrote for each one.

Was there a difference in language used, did you feel one came more from ego than your divine self, could you feel each situation caused a different feeling in different areas of your body, e.g., the challenging situation may have been felt more in your head and stomach, your happy situation may have been more in your heart area?

Did you feel there was a message in either situation?

Did anything around either situation reveal itself as to why it had come into your life?

This kind of exercise is great for getting you to take notice of how you navigate your decisions and reactions, and really help you to get to know yourself.

Chapter 7

The Effects Of Individual and Collective Manifestation

How the individual energy you manifest affects us all and everything in the universe

I remember quite recently seeing a newspaper article and TV coverage describing how two apples were placed in separate jars. One jar was labelled with the word Love and the other labelled with the word Hate.

The apples were left in the jars for a period of time and it was discovered that the apple stored in the jar marked Hate deteriorated and began to rot much faster than the apple stored in the jar labelled with the word Love.

The fact that a jar labelled with a nasty word could influence the deterioration of the apple was met with scepticism and laughter and dismissed as rubbish. This reaction was understandable as no-one explained the process behind the phenomena.

As you may have already worked out, it all came down to energy vibration. The energy vibration of Love, as you will have experienced, has a **very** different feel to the energy vibration of Hate. The energy of Hate is one that manifests as emotions, beliefs and actions of darkness, heaviness, and at worst death and destruction; because of course, everything has a vibrational frequency. The particles that are brought together to form the word Hate have a unique vibration.

Take a moment to feel, experience the vibration of the word Hate. See the word in your mind's eye, say the word out loud, feel the word as an emotion within you. Imagine (don't actually do it), directing thoughts of Hate towards someone you love dearly, it's difficult, you naturally withdraw from wanting to send these thoughts because you 'feel' the energy.

It affects you, right? You feel the vibration of the word, it may only be a word but you can feel the power behind it. You can actually experience a reaction in your physical body, just by thinking of the word; it has an effect.

At this point take a moment to feel the vibration of the word Love, replace any of the previous energy with the positive vibration of Love. See the word Love in your mind's eye, say the word out loud, feel the word as an emotion within you.

Although 'only' words, these words create a very powerful chemical reaction in your body; this is because they are also particles of vibration being brought into form via your instruction.

Words carry energy, sound and frequency.

So, going back to the apple experiment, how would your body cope if you were put in a room and subjected to the energy vibration of Hate for a long period of time? Would you thrive when exposed to Hate continuously, of course you wouldn't.

The apple is no different. When we simply break it down to the world of vibrating particles, and the frequency of the particles, we can see how the negative vibration would affect the vibration of the apple in a negative way, this would then cause the vibration of the apple to change, causing deterioration in its healthy vibrating energy and eventually death.

The lucky Love apple however, would have interacted with the vibration of the word Love, and as a consequence the apple would have had a vibrant, nurturing energy to support its own energy, and would therefore have a healthier and longer lifespan.

No different than we witness in our own health and wellbeing. If you are exposed to Hate, the world is not a nice place to be, you are not going to thrive and have a happy healthy life. The energy of Hate will affect your personal energy vibration, affect your thoughts and emotions and eventually your beliefs and expectations of the world.

When you are exposed to actions, feelings, and words of Love you thrive, you are happy and probably have a longer lifespan. All because the energy behind Love has a beautiful vibration that complements your energy and resonates with it.

If your beliefs are a world of Love and your personal energy, thoughts, and emotions become Love, you 'see' and create beauty and Love in the world.

This is why our world reflects our belief systems and how we feel about ourselves, if we truly understand, connect and love ourselves we embody that energy and emit it to the world. The world is then affected in the same way as the apple; it will thrive and reflect the beauty of the love we feel within, through our expectations and manifestations.

We all share the same space, the same energy and are all intimately, energetically connected, by creation.

I recommend at this point you take a look at the video on YouTube titled "Dr Quantum and Entanglement".

How the energy we manifest affects the individual us

On an individual scale, your world and your reality are a reflection of how you feel about yourself, and a reflection of the programming you have received about yourself and the world.

These programmes that have become your life story so far, are what instruct the world of energy to conform and form your reality.

The design of us as humans, our planet, and the universe is a perfect example of life supporting life on every level. We have been provided with everything to thrive on planet earth, there is nothing missing. Everything is perfection, it's just that ***we have created a distorted view of ourselves, and the world has conformed to our views.***

Your life and everything in it, is like a magic mirror reflecting back at you your beliefs, thoughts, and expectations.

As you now know, your life experience is ***your thoughts made manifest.*** So, think about what is working well in your life, and the beliefs and expectations you have around that area, you can do the same for what is not working so well too.

Sometimes it can take time and practice to get through the initial Ego conclusions and tap into the real thoughts and beliefs at play. As an individual, you don't need to rely on outside direction and explanations to discover your personal world and beyond.

Remember those two words (Love and Hate), and the feelings, reactions, and actions you experienced while manifesting them into your reality. Well, you have just carried out your own experiment, and drawn your own conclusions. Your understanding was experiential, you felt the difference in these two words, and you are drawing your conclusions based on your personal experience (personal empowerment at its best).

The bottom line is that you are in charge at all times. Whatever you see as your reality is a reflection of your thoughts and beliefs.

Our significance and identity has been lost in our human experience, and until we humbly embrace our magnificence as creators and put our creative wizardry into action we will remain stuck in the world of materialistic illusion.

Use your abilities as a creator, and your human reality will manifest into a world of magic and possibilities. You will start to recreate perfection, on every level.

The bonus bit of information

Even after so much information already, I am going to offer up one more piece of fascinating data for you to ponder. I am not going into any depth, at this time, but it is very important you are aware of this research while you are re-establishing your incredible self.

This research points to the real possibility that; ***Information is never destroyed; it exists in all space-time forever.*** [1]

This understanding evolved from the discovery of black holes (a region of space having a gravitational field so intense that no matter or light can escape), and their quantum properties. [1]

Any 'thing' that falls into a black hole, is not destroyed, as once thought. Its information is stored on the 'surface' of the black hole. It is now put forward, with significant scientific experimental evidence to support it, that...[1]

at the centre of each atom is a black hole, and all information, from all time, is contained within every single atom, and atoms are what you and I are made of! [1]

Just ponder on that for a moment, it appears we are made up of atoms that contain all the information, from all time!

Whoa!

[1] Bonny Casel, Quantum Botanicals Course, The Institute of Quantum Botanicals.

A summary of all the science stuff

Let me summarise the amazing stuff we have covered:

- We are all made of tiny particles of vibrating energy, we are beings of vibration.
- This vibrating energy that forms everything is constantly changing, and reacting to its environment.
- This energy reacts to instruction from your consciousness to form matter, and your so-called 'outer world' reality.
- Your personal reality is a reflection of matter coming together according to your beliefs and expectations, via your thoughts and emotions. This is because the observer, that is you, influences how vibrational energy reacts to form matter.
- When broken down into its smallest form, matter is 99.9999999999999% empty space.
- This space is everywhere; we all share the same space.
- You therefore have an effect on the rest of the world via your energy creation and the impact on that shared space.
- Latest research suggests, all atoms have at their centre a black hole that has all information from all time stored within it.
- There is the real possibility, that we all contain all of the information from all time.
- We share the same space and all contain within us the source of all consciousness and creation.

- You, me, the plants, the trees, food, animals, thoughts, emotions, the entire universe is made of vibrating particles of energy.

- This energy is ever present, has no death, only transforms, is full of potential, and is awaiting our conscious instruction, to create.

When we take this information and implement it into our lives, we can live from a completely different perspective, with access to information well beyond just the range of our human senses.

We can begin to approach our life experience with consciousness, fully aware that our consciousness is the true creator of our experiences. Fear, victimhood, insecurities, and lack of significance melt away.

When taking modern physics' description of ourselves, and our world as Vibrational Energy, alongside the ancient description of Life Force Energy or Chi Energy, we are coming to the same conclusion; everything is made of Vibrational Energy.

We are not at the mercy of chance; we are empowered, creative beings, connected to all things, with the wisdom of the universe within us.

Don't Wait Assignment

Your assignment is to take some time out for contemplation, it doesn't matter what time of day, the benefits of reflection time are so important for you.

During this contemplation time, I would like to offer you the opportunity to reflect on the last statement in this chapter (Shown below), reflect on it and feel into it and what it means for you, how it makes you feel, **what new and incredible possibilities it offers you.**

Write the statement and then your thoughts in a journal. You can then refer to them often to build your resilience and personal power, and especially during times of self-doubt, fear or overwhelm.

Your Reflection statement is:

"at the centre of each atom is a black hole, and all information, from all time, is contained within every single atom, and atoms are what I am made of"

"It appears that I am made up of atoms that contain all the information, from all time"!

I truly hope you are beginning to realise your power as a divine, creative, eternal being!

Chapter 8

Ancient Wisdom and Experiential Learning

It is imperative, to work with and grasp this energy theme, because, as you will discover in later chapters, it influences your ***understanding and the outcome of everything***.

Now, further investigating Quantum Physics is great, I completely support research and learning because it will raise questions, and it's these questions that will enable you to expand your boundaries of learning and experience.

However, always be aware that obtaining and unconsciously accepting all your reassurance from external sources can affect the most incredible opportunity of self-discovery and an opportunity to activate your unlimited wisdom.

I did initially try the scientific route to explain my experiences, but felt I was forcing myself to try and understand something I already knew inside, through a language I didn't understand, because the language was not my own.

Once I had worked extensively with Life Force Energy, I tried the scientific route again, feeling I needed to explain my learning, my experiences and newfound wisdom, in a way that would be acceptable to society.

I soon realised I was trying to justify everything I was consciously experiencing through honest self-exploration and learning, via the old programmed habit of seeking approval from external sources and by not trusting the most accurate source of knowledge I have.

Our ***dependence*** on science, has, in my opinion, not always got us to a great place. The work and discoveries science makes in certain areas is phenomenal, but has science (up to this point) given us a healthy connection and understanding of ourselves? I don't believe it has.

Experiential science has now been disregarded. We have lost the ability to discover through experiencing, we have had that right taken away from us due to some of the sciences dismissive approach to anything that is outside the realm of mechanical mathematical measurement, and scientific theory.

The Original, Experiential Wisdom of Life

The indigenous peoples of the world and eastern belief systems never needed science to prove everything they instinctively knew. They never needed an outside scientific source to tell them who they were or where they came from, because they had never lost the connection with their own personal wisdom, their origins, the earth, and the universe.

They knew, without someone telling them in a double-blind study what was within them, they knew that within them, via a now largely forgotten language was the knowledge of the whole universe.

We however, are trying to solve the mysteries of our origins and our true nature, with what appear to them very odd methods.

Those looking down from a place of seeing the whole, must be flabbergasted by our blindness. You will never have better proof than your own personal discoveries, because as you now know you have the knowledge of the universe within you.

Interestingly, some of the world's leading scientists including Einstein, W. Heisenberg, Werner and Nikola Tesla acknowledged that much of what science was re-discovering in Quantum Physics was in fact already known about and recorded in Ancient Indian Sanskrit Texts.

Werner Heisenberg, stated:

"After conversations about Indian Philosophy, some of the ideas of Quantum Physics that had seemed crazy suddenly made more sense." [2]

I completely encourage you to look further into science and self-development, as this will trigger deep questioning and self-discovery.

It will also enable you to become more open to the specific information you need, as you will intuitively attract the books or resources (via your own conscious energy creation) that best serve you at that moment.

---

[2] Werner Heisenberg – German Theoretical Physicist. Born 5th December 1901, Died 1st February 1976. Won the Nobel Prize for Physics in 1932.

Everything I am writing about I have found within myself, firstly and most importantly by living consciously, with awareness and ***real self-honesty***. By being open to learn from the wisdom of others and also by being aware of and open to learn from, an intuitive guidance outside of my restricted human perception.

This, my fellow explorers, is the toughest but most accurate, double, triple, quadruple blind experiment I have ever done. The truth you get from yourself will never ever leave you and with intention, will only grow. You will regain an unwavering calm and wisdom, which will be your ticket to a fearless and completely fulfilling life.

Another well placed quote, at this point, by Werner Heisenberg is: "The reality we can put into words is never reality itself".[4]

You have to feel it, experience it and consciously create it.

Experiencing your first empowered, conscious, energy, experiential experiment!

The indigenous people and many eastern belief systems always knew that everything in the universe is connected in some way. They knew that ourselves, and everything around us, is made up of a living, constantly changing life force that connects and affects everything in the universe.

[4] The Genie in your Genes, Book by Dawson Church

They knew this long before science came along, because they experienced it, ***they allowed themselves the time to reflect, contemplate and were not overwhelmed by a world of distractions.*** They stayed connected to and fully aware of their own and the universes life force energy, the Interconnectedness of everything, and the knowledge of eternal life.

This is a crucial area, where we have come to solely rely on external sources. We rely on others interpretations, restricted by their personal beliefs, human perceptions and senses, to tell us who and what we are. Much of what science is now beginning to 'prove' really is going full circle, back to the original knowing of these 'wise ones'.

Always remember, we have become limited by our five senses and human vocabulary but our ability to experience through consciousness and intuition is limitless.

So, as a being without limits, I want you to discover this universal energy for yourself. Play and have fun drawing on what is actually you, because this energy I am referring to is the foundation of your whole existence.

I would like you to have the opportunity to become your own scientist, your own wise one. You can connect to this vibrating energy, for yourself, right now.

The more you practice, the more sensitive you become to detecting and feeling your own and the life force of everything around you.

Don't Wait Assignment

Firstly, gently turn your ***intention*** towards feeling/sensing energy (remember your intention creates), at the same time just be open to experience, have no expectations or fixed outcome. This is about being in the moment.

If possible, but by no means essential, find a space with limited distractions. Become still, quiet and relaxed. Take some gentle deep breaths and relax your body.

1. Sit comfortably with your arms bent at your sides, palms facing each other. Set the intention in your mind and heart that you are going to feel your life force energy.

2. Rub your hands together vigorously for about 5 seconds. Then hold your hands approximately 5 inches apart and hold them there for a minute.

3. Keeping the arms bent in the same position, try moving your hands back and forth slightly. The width of someone's energy field will define how far apart your hands need to be, so experiment. The area where you see a dip in your palms is generally the most sensitive area but energy can be felt anywhere on the hand.

4. You may feel heat, cold, tingles, but most commonly a feeling of slight resistance can be detected.

5. You may feel nothing at first but with practice you will.

6. It is also great to carry out this exercise with someone else. Follow the instructions above but sit facing each other with their palms facing yours. Tune into each other's energy, you may well be amazed.

Don't just limit this energy practice to yourself and others. Try it with plants, animals, food and water. The more you practice the more you will sense the many different vibrations that make up our world.

This experiment helps to demonstrate there is a life force present in and around all of us, that has massive potential to expand your understanding of everything.

Chapter 9

Meet your Divine bit... The Primary Self

No more separation anxiety - coming home to the real you.

Just before you read the coming paragraphs, I would like to take a moment to remind you of how I described myself in the early chapters of this book; an ordinary girl living an ordinary life. No special known gifts to give me a head start in understanding all this stuff.

As I began to proof read this and previous chapters I realised, the information I am sharing may come across as far removed from what you have been taught, and conditioned to believe about yourself.

There is a danger your Ego will over complicate things in your head and you may even just skim over the words, because you believe this information doesn't relate to you, it's not relevant to you (oh, but it is), or on first glance you don't understand, so you move on.

The Ego may also have you believe this information is coming from someone way off your level, someone who somehow knows way more than you ever could.

Bear in mind, these thoughts can even be unconscious, you may not even realise you have shut off from the words, and the meaning they have for you.

I am not in a different place to you, I am not detached from you, I wasn't handed this on a plate, but what I do have (unknowingly, in the early days) is inside knowledge. I just had to tap into it.

As you now know, I have inside knowledge, ***just like you do***. We are no different in our ability to rediscover the truth of ourselves, I am me and you are you, but ultimately this is about us.

As you read on, please read consciously, don't over complicate things, because it really is not complicated. Trust yourself and know, without question, you have the very same inside knowledge as me. You just need to ***listen out for it,*** and then ***listen to it.***

So, with your confident, wide-awake, 'this is totally relevant to me' head on, here we go…

When we take the modern-day physics description of ourselves as Vibrational Energy (tiny vibrating particles) and the ancient description of Life Force Energy, we come to the same conclusion. Everything is made of Energy.

To remind you of what we covered in Chapter 4,

Energy that:

- ***Is constantly vibrating***
- ***Cannot be destroyed***
- ***Only ever changes its form***
- ***Has the ability to manifest form under our instruction***
- ***Appears to have within it, all the information, from all time***

So, from this perspective you might wonder how can we just be this human body?

If we are made up of tiny particles of Energy, that only change form, and have no death, what are we before we have a physical body, and what are we after our physical body ceases to function/ exist?

Ready to jump into another deep end for the answer?

Each one of us is living a 'man'-ufactured existence. An existence that requires us to outsource ourselves in order to fit in with the false expectations we have created as our world.

We repeat unhealthy patterns of human behaviour and co- dependency in order to feed and recreate what is familiar. But at some point, most of us have a flicker, a moment, months, or even years wondering, is this it?

My serious questioning began in 1997. At that point I realised I had to take a leap of faith, take a step back from the familiarity and influences of our 'man'-ufactured society.

Firstly, I had to establish a relationship with myself, so I could personally activate, and create my reality myself from within. Create health and harmony from within, create a healthy economy from within, and learn my purpose for being here from within. I had to remember who I was, dig through all the created goo, face all my uglies, and spring clean everything.

I share with you what I discovered, through honest and at times very challenging work; I share information that comes from a place of truth.

I share from a point of personal exploration and excavation, and the privilege of sharing others' personal experiences.

So, to answer the original question of, 'who is the real you', here goes...

Our Human self is simply an ***aspect of the total energy of who we are.***

The ***main mass of vibrational energy,*** which I refer to as our ***Primary Conscious Self,*** is our ***ever present, immortal, authentic, conscious, intuitive Divine Self.***

Our human suits are created as a result of an instruction/ intention from our Primary Conscious Self (our consciousness), to form matter at the correct vibration to exist and experience life on earth.

As you now know, you are a creator; Energy conforms to your conscious instruction, and expectations.

The intuitive feelings, wisdom and knowing that you experience within your personal internal human environment, is your ***Primary Consciousness*** in place.

Your human form is energy, energy that is at this very moment (as always) connected to the energy of your Primary Conscious Self. In other words, you are always connected to yourself. Your Primary Self is not in some faraway place, but holds its place in the universe, while your human aspect is experiencing life on earth.

Your human form is just ***One Vibrational Energy Expression of who you are,*** you are a mass of vibrating energy, energy vibrating at different frequencies according to its environment and its purpose, you [insert your name here] are part of your Primary Conscious Self at all times because you are your Primary Conscious Self at all times.

You are not exclusively human. Your human self is simply an aspect of you, produced and manifested by you, your Primary Conscious Self.

You are your Primary Conscious Self, you are part of everything, and within you is the wisdom of all time.

You <u>are</u> identity, significance and love.

I recommend you reread, now or later, the last paragraphs. Take some time to think about the information. What does it mean or represent to you? How does it make you feel? Do you feel resistance or relief at being offered this information?

Think about each point, but think with your heart, feel from within, and only take what feels right for you at this time. Also be aware, what may not connect with you now, may well connect and make perfect sense tomorrow, in a week, or next year.

Your Human Aspect comes fully equipped for the journey

You are blessed with the most incredible vehicle, a physical body, to transport you through your human experience. You have created an aspect of yourself, a physical human body, made up ofenergy vibrating at a compatible speed to enable you to exist on earth.

While having your human experience, you have a constant connection and communication with your Primary Conscious (Energy) Self. This communication holds the information of all that you are, and all details relating to your human experience. You can be in conscious control of your life by clearing and keeping your lines of communication with your Conscious Self open, and following your own guidance.

It seems completely crazy to think we would arrive on this planet with no guidance, no instruction book, and no manual! Just landing here and left to get on with it.

How can that possibly be the case, when the earth, everything that inhabits it, and the whole universe has their own way of thriving and functioning (without our help).

Everything in the universe, except us (it appears), is aware of, and is connected to, its own inner knowledge and guidance.

Everything around us uses its inbuilt Consciousness and Intelligence to create and thrive. We do not instruct the sun to rise every morning; it naturally works in conjunction with the rotation of the earth to give us, and our planet, light. The leaves naturally fall in autumn, the tree and flower buds have a conscious inbuilt intelligence guiding them to grow in spring, and animals know when and how to adapt to the changing seasons.

There are many factors involved in these processes, all achieved through the universal language of energy interaction, and staying connected to their inside intelligence and knowledge.

Realise, you have not been left out of this process. You were born aware of your inner knowledge and connection to the big stuff. It has just been conditioned out of you. You absolutely do have your own inside knowledge, via your Primary Conscious Self.

Just look around you, the universe is perfection, nature is perfection, birth is perfection, the seasons are perfection, the plants are perfection, the animals are perfection, and us, we are perfection too, but we have become blind to it, simply because we see ourselves as purely human, and detached from the natural world.

Why on earth would we be within the universe and separate from it? Everything within the universe is part of the universe, and apart from us, appears to know its place within it too.

It makes no sense at all, that we would be the only 'things' on this planet, within the universe, that are completely separate.

The fact is we are not separate, everything is from the same source of creation and until we start to realise, accept, and reintegrate ourselves back into universal society, we will stay in our own prison cells of materialistic, unfulfilled existence.

We need to wake up to the fact that our human-based, isolated existence, is not working. We now have to look within ourselves to find our own inner guidance and wisdom, which everything else on this planet has and operates from.

It is time for us to lose the amnesia, take responsibility, learn, and understand how to reconnect with the inner guidance of our Primary Conscious Self, and reintegrate back into universal society.

How we used to be

Prior to our state of amnesia, a respect existed for our natural world, because we were aware we were from the same source of creation. We never considered ourselves separate or superior. Instead, we worked together with nature and animals, we had a mutually beneficial, and respectful relationship, because we knew everything was interconnected.

Our consciousness and inner intelligence ensured a continued connection to our Primary Conscious Self, our origins, and our abilities as creative beings.

This connection also meant there was never any separation between loved ones in human form, and those who had 'died' and transformed their human body (more on this later).

We do not disappear after the energy vibration of our physical body changes, as you now know our energy is deathless.

At death, we are still that same vibrational energy, that same Primary Consciousness; we have just transformed the heavier, denser part of us that formed our physical body.

Everyone's Primary Conscious Self, always remains connected in the universe, through energy interaction and communication.

This connection gives us the ability to be aware of our 'whole' self, and our connection to everything.

The Energy that is our Primary Conscious Self means we always hold our place in the universe, and we have all the necessary abilities, via our Primary Self, to communicate with loved ones who no longer occupy their human form, via conscious energy interaction.

This is also true for nature and the whole universe; we have all the necessary abilities to communicate with everything.

When we donned our human suits, and began to play out our existence here, we were always connected to our origins, via the energy intelligence of our Primary Conscious Self.

We are part of the consciousness that created everything, and that consciousness created your Primary Self that supplied you with the skills to have physical, mental, and emotional intelligence, while in human form. We did not land here without guidance, separated, and cut off from everything.

Alongside all our incredible human abilities, we have all the guidance and wisdom we could ever need, via connection to our Primary Conscious Self.

Our human physical senses, combined with the connection to our Primary Conscious Self, enables us to be fully aware, at all times, of our identity and significance.

These same gifts also enable us to experience life on earth, and grow through connection with other people, the natural world, and the universe.

Your Primary Self, your consciousness, can be experienced through your inner world, experienced as your quiet voice of experience, your intuition, a feeling, an instinct, an inner knowing.

That is the voice of your conscious self and is where all your answers can be found.

Don't Wait Assignment

It's time to get to know your whole self. This chapter offers you the understanding that whatever is happening in the world you always have the comfort, security, and power to know that you are *always* connected to that part of you that holds all the wisdom from all time within. Your primary self is the constant by your side, through everything and is always available to you, because it is you.

So, I offer you the opportunity to place yourself in a space of relaxation, allow your body to sink into a state of softness, then take your attention to your heart, settle into that *beautiful seat of wisdom and knowing.* In this space treat it as a meditation, a quiet place to retreat, feel the softness, the colours, the certainty, and strength that is found here, and then allow this energy to flow out into the rest of your body.

Reflect on how this space feels, what you find there, get to know the feeling, the wisdom, the voice of your Primary Self that lives here.

It can take you in an incredible life direction, because *only you know you*, and this is the part of you that you have been missing all your life.

This space is the place to come home to You, home to the universe, and lose the insecurities, fear, and lack that this separation has created for you.

This is where you make your world better, you live in the world, not dependent on it to get better, you live in the world on your terms connected to your whole self.

Do this regularly, as a daily practice, and expand on it as you allow your intuition to guide you into a longer or more expanded experience.

Chapter 10

The Forgotten Language Of The Universe

While the language of humanity sets boundaries, the unspoken universal language of energy creates depths of experience, beyond any words.

We now have scientific awareness of our energy make up, an energy that is deathless, and only ever changes form. We have all been aware at some point of a higher guidance, an intuitive prompt; why would this not come from your Primary Conscious Self?

Maybe because, it doesn't fit into our current model of acceptable modern-day science, or socially acceptable theories?

This vibrational energy, and conscious awareness of its existence, is exactly what gave the indigenous people of the world that vital connection to everything, and such deep wisdom, knowledge, and identity.

In my experience, ***this vibrational energy, this life force energy is the forgotten language that explains and connects everything in our universe.***

This energy is the lost language that creates the connection between mediums, and the 'deceased', and the moments when you feel a loved one is near.

This energy is the lost language behind a feeling of love, gratitude, and joy that is experienced but cannot be truly communicated using our human words.

This energy is the forgotten language, which creates spontaneous healing, through a deeper connection that goes beyond modern day understanding.

This energy is the forgotten language that is felt in the presence of nature, no words are exchanged as the sea communicates with us, to lift our spirits.

This energy is the forgotten language we experience when walking in nature, the connection and communication from trees that offer us clarity in times of turmoil.

This energy is the forgotten language felt when we experience a feeling towards others that says, "I feel comfortable in your presence", but no words are spoken.

This energy is the forgotten language we hear in times of trauma, when we are brought to that quiet place, when anything unimportant is pushed aside, to leave space for us to hear ourselves.

This energy is the forgotten language, a whisper, a feeling, that is calling you to look for a better way, a better life, a life of meaning, and understanding.

This energy is the forgotten language of energy communication between your Primary Conscious Self, and your human self.

This energy is the forgotten language, the common bond that connects everything in the universe.

We experience so much in our world through feeling, inner knowing, and intuitive guidance.

This is the language of energy. This, my friend, is consciousness.

Don't Wait Assignment

Simply spend today noticing the language of energy. Become aware of how your environment makes you feel, especially pay attention to nature, whether it's a pot plant in an apartment, the trees in a park, the sea, a view, the sky.

Go through your day aware of how the different environments you find yourself in make you feel. Whether it's at home, in nature, an office, or shopping etc. See what you find in those spaces feeling wise.

Record your feelings in a journal and start to notice how certain environments 'talk' to you without using language. This not only helps you to retune yourself to speaking with and hearing the universe and the earth, it also helps you to notice which environments support you to thrive and which ones may not.

Happy exploring!

Chapter 11

How Did We Become So Disconnected From Ourselves And Universal Society?

Why did everything go silent?

Many regard the suggestion of anything outside society's acceptable view of our material existence as suspicious. It is regarded with suspicion because our ability to remember has been so buried under layers of the dense, heavy, energy of human emotion.

Our lack of identity, feelings of insignificance, and all other miscreated human emotions, were created by some of our greatest human abilities. Abilities that have led us down a very different path from the one we were originally on.

The human abilities I refer to include, free will, free thought, and choice.

In human form we have the ability to make informed decisions and choices. Gradually, through human history, our motivation to make decisions using our own personal free will changed.

It changed from creating and living by shared respected values and understanding - values and understandings that kept us connected to our Primary Conscious Self.

We changed because we began using our free will, thoughts, and decisions to our own individual benefit, without regard for the whole. With no regard for the interconnectedness of all life here on earth, and within the universe.

This change can be seen throughout history in the way we began to treat each other, treat the natural world, and produce a hierarchy system that reflected our individual status based on material wealth or power.

Many points in human history can be seen to support this need to compete for status and create separation through systems of human hierarchy. The more recent hierarchy systems meant the days of having a 'leader' who has gained respect because of their experience, wisdom, and respect for the whole faded away.

It was replaced by a society that admired personal wealth, and material success as something to aspire to.

This was more recently reinforced by modern day science teaching us that knowledge and wisdom that came from our observations, connection to our environment, and our personal experiences are anecdotal and unreliable, because it is based on personal account rather than 'facts' or 'research'. In other words, your opinion, conclusions, and experiences have become invalid. This view is completely disempowering and contributes greatly to our personal insecurities and insignificance.

And so, down the slippery slope we began to slide. From this point many of us became more and more focused on personal human gain to satisfy their need for identity and significance.

This then led to actions of selfishness and disconnection from others, the natural world and the universe. Most seriously, this meant disconnection from our Primary Consciousness Selves, our inner intelligence, wisdom, and guidance.

The more that humans become focused on personal gain, the more detached they become from their own identity, and the natural environment.

This behaviour produced lower emotions; ***our internal dialogue changed.*** These negative emotions arose as a result of fear, produced through selfish acts without consideration for the whole, that then left us lost.

We lost our place in the world and in turn lost our Identity, Significance, and Self Love.

Our negative emotions formed dense energy within our human form, which clouded our view of who we are, and we began to seek more and more satisfaction from personal gain in our human world, because we had less and less security and identity from within.

Eventually, we could no longer hear the inner voice that had connected us on such a deep and sacred level to everything.

As humans, we no longer exist with a deep love and respect for all things. We no longer exist with a deep love for ourselves, and our origins.

We no longer have the ability to communicate with the earth, the universe, and our loved ones.

Most crucially, we no longer have a clear connection to our Primary Conscious Self. The Primary Conscious Self that is our authentic self, and holds all the wisdom and information we will ever need, the energy that holds within it our deepest understanding of everything.

We have clogged up our lines of communication with the dense, heavy, energy vibration of miscreated human emotion. We have replaced intuition with Ego, and we can no longer hear ourselves, we can no longer feel the security of our 'home', and the guidance of our authentic Self.

We exist in fear, because we are lost, lost in a place that does not reflect who we are.

The more humanity focuses solely on their human existence and the material world, the more detached from our authentic selves we become. The more detached we become the more we produce these dense emotions of fear and insignificance.

As a consequence, we now only see through our limited human perception. Now, our eyes only 'see' a purely materialistic human world.

We have created many tools to reinforce our belief in a solely materialistic existence, such as relying solely on scientific evidence, money motivated identity and the constant busyness that disconnects us from ourselves.

We have quite literally reprogrammed our 'vision' of the whole, into the 'blindness' of human existence via learnt behaviour and thought patterns, and their subsequent expectations.

It is now known that what the human brain receives through observation is highly selective, and is based on information that ***has already created a pathway within the brain***. So, when you have repetitive thought processes over and over you create these inroads in your brain and new information is ***quite literally 'invisible'*** to your brain, until something happens to make it visible. ***You only see what you have programmed yourself to see.***

Your consciousness has the ability to comprehend so much more than the limited interpretations you have carved out for yourself. You carve out pathways, through repetitive thinking and expectations, and as we now know vibrational energy (matter) alters its behaviour when it is observed or measured; you get the results you are focusing on. You the observer and the observed cannot be separated. Matter reacts to your expectations.

From this viewpoint, our energetic information blueprint that enables us to experience life in human form (while still entwined with our Conscious Self), has literally been overlaid with the highly dense vibrational goo of our complex and miscreated human emotions.

This is how we have become such highly complex, fearful, emotional human beings, and why we constantly seek out Identity and Significance via our 'man'-ufactered world, and it is what causes our lack of Self Love.

This is why, up to this moment, you have been lost, looking to your material world for your Self and your Identity. Literally blocked off from you.

But **today** all that changes. You realise your origins, your connection to everything, and the fact that you are an extraordinary and creative being.

You need to carve out new pathways in the brain, using this new understanding of your creative abilities. Create new thought processes and expectations to create your and our world anew.

The more you use conscious decision and transform programmed belief systems, you transform the dense energy of miscreated emotion, and replace it with new lighter energy that enables you to clear a path to once again hear yourself.

You will create different expectations of your life and how the world looks to you. In turn the world of energy conforms to manifest your new expectations.

Your Authentic, Primary Conscious Self is still there, with all its possibilities, just waiting for you to remember, and from the moment of intention, recognition or remembering, the reconnection is absolutely possible.

From the moment you have the desire or intention to start the process of connecting to your Authentic Self, the energy of the universe, under your instruction, begins to manifest whatever you need to start the process; your intention has an energetic frequency that will produce an action. The reconnection begins.

Don't Wait Assignment

This is short and sweet, *but oh so powerful.* Using the energy of intention to create, I invite you to use the following statement to bring your original blueprint of creatorship and connection to the surface, to retrieve it from the layers of human emotion that it has been stuck under for so very long.

Use this everyday… because as you now know, intention is an instruction to produce that which you are consistently focused on.

"I now active my original blueprint of divine perfection and creation. I now dissolve all lower emotions that have been keeping my blueprint of perfection in the darkness, and I see the radiant, gleaming, luminous, light of my original divine blueprint coming into clear vision.

As I connect to the wisdom of the universe and to the grace that is my true home, I become my whole divine self"

And so it is.

Chapter 12

If You Are Not Your Authentic Self, Who Are You?

No offence, but you are a right old mishmash of beliefs and behaviours!

For so many generations we have been living with our disconnection from our origins, and with every generation we have passed down to the next generation the same distorted view of life and our existence.

If you take a moment to look at your view of the world, you will be able to trace the origins of your emotional characteristics and behaviour back to the information you were given and processed about the world during your childhood.

As an adult you are already programmed to form opinions and react to life's experiences in a certain way, and these emotions and behaviours are reinforced by society and become ingrained as your truth.

You were given a view of the world based on others reactions to their loss of identity, and all the deep-seated fears and emotionally complex behaviours this brought about.

This is not a criticism of the people who you encountered in your childhood, but an acknowledgement of what they were taught and what the past generations taught each other.

Please do not take this lightly, I am referring to the many emotion's we humans carry around - fear, anger, insecurities, lack of self-love, a need to control, a fear of lack, a need for identity, a need for significance, and a need for love.

These disruptive emotions and behaviours are not real, yes, they appear real because that is what you have been taught makes up your world. Your expectations make them 'real'.

Your emotions and behaviour patterns, have been created by others, over centuries and generations of others distorted views, taken on by you. Currently, to a great degree, they suffocate your true existence, they have become your reality.

You continue to reinforce these emotions and behaviour patterns, using your expectations (or should I say others expectations you have taken on) to manifest your reality. Your internal programming reproduces the same patterns of creation daily, without youeven realising.

This is where inaccurate quotes such as "it runs in the family", "I'm just like my mother", "it's hereditary" reinforce repetitive trans-generational behaviour patterns that affect every aspect of your life, from health and relationships, to how we see ourselves, and how we interpret the world around us.

Please remember your life is all about learnt behaviour patterns creating your reality, according to your expectations. Your fate is not solely reliant on the story that has become your family history. Your fate, your reality is created in the moment using **your** thoughts and expectations.

Whether it is your conscious thoughts or unconscious pre- programmed behaviour patterns that create your life, is up to you.

As I shared at the beginning of this book, listed here are a few of the common side effects (of which I experienced at least 99% of at some point) of living by learnt behaviour and a false identity:

- Fear (very, very, few people live without some kind of fear)
- Anxiety
- Depression
- Worry
- Panic
- Stress
- Pushing yourself too hard
- Striving hard towards goals at the expense of your wellbeing
- Boredom
- Insecurities
- Lack of confidence
- Lack of self-love
- Lack of self-care

These symptoms appear because you have taken on others identity, other people's views of the world, and other people's stuff.

It is other people's stuff; it is not yours. You no longer need to suffer stress, anxiety, and fear trying to achieve what is not attainable outside yourself.

What produces these complex emotional reactions, is you, ***because you are trying to live someone else's life, in fact many people's lives!***

As you live via your learnt behaviour and inaccurate view of the world, on some level these views feel irrational to you.

As a consequence you then feel out of control, you have no true identity because you are living as someone else.

Living by someone else's truth, produces feelings of lack of Identity, Insignificance and lack of Self Love. All created because you are disconnected from yourself, and you are trying to live through others views of the world. You are trying to live as your past.

To end this chapter, I will leave you with these life changing words, that you can now see as truth.

YOU ARE NOT YOUR PAST
Unless you choose to reside there

Don't Wait Assignment

Repeat, and write in your journal…

"I am not my past, unless I choose to reside there"

You are here, you are reading, learning, exploring, questioning, and choosing creatorship!

You my friend are choosing to reclaim your birth right, your creatorship, and the miraculous life you are here to live! For that I salute you!

Chapter 13

Awesome Creations

The practicalities of becoming your Authentic Self

So, now you have all this lovely, fresh information. What do you do with it? How do you put it into practice? How do you move through your mishmash of baggage and reconnect with your conscious self?

1. Build on the previous chapters. Consider your new understanding of you, and your abilities as a creative being.

2. Use all the following chapters to learn how to transform yourself, into 'you', by understanding the whole, and connecting the missing links to become empowered.

The process of becoming your authentic self is about incorporating every aspect of our human life on earth, and grasping how it affects and supports us. Combine that with living **consciously,** listening, acting on your intuition, your internal truth and brushing the voice of doubt/Ego off your shoulder when it perches itself there.

This is about empowerment through knowledge, understanding, and ultimately having the tools to confidently step up to embrace your world, your human life, your passing, your eternal existence, your connection to everything, and ultimately your power as a creative being, from a perspective of true understanding, gratitude and unwavering truth.

What you have read so far may now need some time to settle in. On the one hand the information can feel familiar; it feels right on some level. On the other hand, it could be so far away from what you have been taught, it can initially seem difficult to know how it will fit into your current life and belief system.

Therefore, if you feel the need, give yourself some time to re-read and process what you have learnt so far.

If it is important to you, and connects with you, you owe yourself the time to really feel the energy of the information, and let it settle. You will then bring into your life what your conscious self/ intuition knows is right for you.

What you take into your heart is the beginning of the new you; the real you. This fresh information brings about new thoughts and emotions, which will replace old outdated ones.

Now, as you continue your journey as a Recovering Insignificant Human ☺, you need to be aware of what reinforces the old you and what presents itself as an opportunity to become the best version of you. The coming chapters will cover exactly this.

If you are ready to step up, the rewards and gems you uncover will be beyond incredible, and your life will never ever be the same.

As you learn how to rediscover yourself, experience has taught me it is the most rewarding process **ever**, but also not the easiest, not the prettiest, and takes perseverance. Please be prepared for some beautiful highs and also some sticky lows.

As you release what is not you, you will see the complex human emotions you have created for what they are - unnecessary and unreal. When you see the truth of life, you lose all fear and pain.

You will have all your needs met on every level, with ease.

You can tap into a whole team of support via your (for the moment) unseen friends and family, all the lovelies who have shed their human suits but are right there cheering for you.

Life really can be incredible, every moment, every day. The more of us who embrace and transform what is not the authentic us, will collectively influence the energy and expectations of the world, and together we will co-create an incredible ***global human existence;*** it is a team effort that starts with you.

Creating the best life ever, is completely possible, but like anything, you have to become familiar with your new job, your new role, and go through some re-training until it becomes second nature.

For example, I am writing a book as a result of studying human potential for over 20 years. I know my subject matter because I have studied, questioned, learnt, questioned, worked, questioned, experienced, questioned and walked the walk.

I could not arrive in a courtroom tomorrow and do the job of a highly qualified barrister. I have no experience, and no training. I would need to learn a whole new trade.

In the same way, you won't necessarily wake up tomorrow and be a fully conscious, telepathic, wise being, free of all human issues, and be totally enlightened (although I have learnt to never say never)!

You understand where I am coming from? You need to learn how to be yourself again. Learn your subject, practice and implement it. You need to learn how to practically manage your empowerment while staying grounded and still living your human existence.

There are incredible people doing amazing things in the world, who can provide you with oodles of support during this process, myself being included.

Also, the people and resources that 'randomly' appear once you show up to do your thing, is magical.

Let the retraining commence!

The following chapters will cover the main internal and external influences in your life, that influence and control your everyday thoughts, emotions, and actions, that in turn impact your view of yourself and the world.

I offer you another view about the often outdated and unhelpful messages behind many of the biggest influences in all our lives, and how they reinforce our inauthentic materialist views and keep us in the same cycle, recreating the same reality.

To pre warn you, when you read and digest the following chapters, your Ego will almost certainly be waiting at the starting line. It may even have a full-on toddler tantrum, presenting you with thoughts such as:

- Why am I even reading this?
- What a load of rubbish?
- I don't want to change anyway?
- I can't!
- I'm nervous!
- I'm far too busy!
- I'm not clever enough!
- People will think I'm mad!
- I'm not well enough!
- It's not relevant to me!
- I'll start to incorporate this information into my life, just not right now!

You know the sort of thing. The more you feel the information could be relevant, the bigger the resistance can become.

In my experience, the information contained in this book can challenge everything in your world, and all you have been taught.

But it can also be the route towards a life more wonderful than you can currently even imagine… so let's do it anyway.

Don't Wait Assignment

Now the fun and adventures really begin with the practicalities of you becoming your whole self… you have so got this!

As you move into the second part of this Book, just make sure the ego volume is turned down, and your intuition is turned up.

Stay aware of where your mind is taking you, and if necessary, repeat our original statement of "May my mind thoughts be replaced by my Divine thoughts".

Let's do this!

Chapter 14

Moving Into The Next Stage Of The Book

The reality may now be setting in, that this book is not just another self-help book.

This book is not about fixing who you have become, it is about reconnecting you to you.

Then, you can realise, and work with your absolute divine power as a creative being.

Ultimately, the whole purpose of this book is for me to share with you everything I can, in order for you to rediscover your magnificence as a creative being. To once again learn to trust yourself and your own wisdom implicitly, and trust the process of life, death, and beyond. For anyone questioning any area of their life, the crucial ***first step***, without exception, is to embrace the information in this book and begin living it.

I want for you to once again connect with yourself and the wider world from a place of self-belief, respect, and reverence. I want you to take action that makes a positive contribution, and to trust the process of life, death, and beyond.

I want you to be happy, healthy, wise and free of fear. I want you to consciously create your heart's (not your Ego's) desire, and I want you to live your purpose.

The remaining chapters offer you the information for the next steps, to get you to where you want to be. The next chapter in particular is fundamental to accessing your own personal guidance to reclaim your power and perfection. It will help you to easily identify opportunities to bring balance back into your life and get you on the road to meeting your authentic self.

It is my firm belief that you will never fully reach your purpose or potential without incorporating the essence of who you are. How can you, using only the surface level information of personal development and lifestyle change? ***This approach simply treats the symptoms of who you have become, and does not work with the core of who you are.***

As always this process starts with you, you can create all you need from within and have all the tools to start right here, right now.

The most important thing in your life, is to learn to understand who you are, then all the great resources' and information such as nutrition, personal development, finance, science, relationships, and spirituality will be incorporated into your life.

These will be based upon the solid foundation of your true self, not your miscreated Ego self that wavers through uncertainty and lack of identity. The real You who is in charge from a point of grace, at all times.

Even when you have wobbles through this process, because you will, it's natural, you still have the underlying strength of knowing it is your birthright to create, it is the energy blueprint of who you are.

You are a creator.

During periods of self-doubt, you have the knowledge that we all have the same starting points, and the same magnificence, it just comes down to who questions, who steps up, and who starts to use their 'magical' creative powers.

So, even during the wobbles, you can still stand strong in your knowledge and power as the incredible being that you are.

I don't know how I can stress any further, how utterly incredible every one of us is, how incredible this opportunity of life is.

It is the single, biggest, and most precious gift we could have.

Please, if the time is right for you, be bold, step up, and embrace this information. Laugh, cry, scream and dance through the process of discovering yourself. It is all part of the experience of life, and all part of the process.

Embrace it, live it, and you will have a life beyond anything you can yet imagine.

Don't wait Assignment

As we move into the practicalities of becoming your authentic, divine, whole self, now would be a good time to remind yourself of what you want your life to look like, do you want to build a calling or a mission, manifest your heart's desire, serve others, have more fun, more peace, more self-love/care, a wonderful relationship, something else, or all of the above and more?

When you anchor in your reason/s for doing something that may require some focus, you will approach it with more determined action, a place of certainty that you will achieve it, and a mindset that is open, and naturally manifests the opportunities and support that you require.

So, write down in your journal all you would like to achieve/experience in life, no holding back, remember anything is possible, big, small, or huge, write it all down. Then put it in order of heart importance (not head/ego/fear importance) and then remind yourself that you have come fully equipped for this human journey to create everything you want to experience.

You can glance back at this list at any time, you can change and update it at any time, and you can use it to remind yourself of your desires and creatorship.

You can also use this list to notice what 'feels right' to move forward with, to start taking steps to create something. Often when you list something that is high on the list of heart importance (i.e., feels right), it may not make any logical sense and yet you just know it feels right... that is your divine guidance, no forcing, pushing, stressing to make it happen, it is in line with your life plan so 'feels' right.

Chapter 15

No More Insignificant You, Let's Get The Magnificent You Back

Using your personal mirror to see

As the subtitle suggests, as always, ***you*** have your very own personal guidance to help you figure it all out, and this is where we will start. Start by using the opportunities you present yourself with (your mirror), to see what is not authentically you.

It can be daunting to start the whole self-discovery process, but eventually you will know yourself so well, being with yourself will be the most comfortable and secure place to be in the whole world.

This mirror I am referring to, is the mirror that ***reflects your internal world via your external experience of life***. This mirror shows you exactly what is holding you back from being your authentic self. This mirror will show you everything that needs to be transformed.

How does this Mirror work?

Your internal environment - your thoughts, feelings, emotions, and beliefs in the world, all carry their own individual energy frequencies that manifest into stuff, your 'external' life experiences.

Everything you are experiencing as your life (your external world) is a manifestation of your internal world.

Your experience of life mirrors back to you your beliefs about everything including; relationships, work, money, health, and the world around you.

Your current reality has been created by your internal world, NOT by your external world.

The external world manifests in order to support your beliefs, authentic or not. The world will only manifest according to your beliefs, and these are the instructions energy needs to manifest your world into form.

This is where the mirror effect comes in. Whatever you are experiencing in your life now, in every moment, is where you will find the clues to what is **not** authentically you.

For example, if you have challenges with money, there will be some kind of restricting belief system that has been instilled in you, regarding money and abundance.

Lack of self-love and lack of self-worth signifies you are carrying the energy of a belief from something you experienced that gave you a distorted view of yourself, and you continue to carry that belief with you.

That same belief may now be manifesting in your reality in the form of others not treating you with love and respect. It is not that you are a bad person, it just means you need to be aware and honest with yourself, and clear the distorted beliefs about yourself.

When you encounter anything that is unbalanced in your reality (unbalanced emotions, reactions, actions and life circumstances), ***these circumstances will always be fuelled by distorted information about yourself or the world which has become part of your belief system, and expectations of life.***

All your beliefs and internal programming will be reflected via your personal life circumstances, because the energy vibration of those beliefs instructs energy potential to form your world.

Using your personal life circumstances as your accurate guide to uncovering everything that does not belong to you, is perfection. You are your own guide; you use your own wisdom. It works even if you have no idea what distorted beliefs you have in place, you are constantly pointing them out to yourself via your personal circumstances.

You are a creator! Inherited distorted beliefs will play out in the form of how we experience the world; you create your world according to your expectations!

I wonder, did you have any idea how empowered you already are? How you are in no way a victim of life but the true creator of your story?

How to support the process of finding and releasing your inauthentic bits

As you really start to embark on the course of self-discovery, you need some tools, tools that will be the main keys to success. These tools are uncomplicated, available at all times, and under your control at all times.

You need to use them consistently until they become automatic. From now, read these four points, keep them in the forefront of your mind, write them down, post-it note the house, work with them, and never forget them, ever.

1. ***Awareness:*** become really aware of everything that goes on ***within you*** and ***within your reality*** (external circumstances). Become aware of ***your thoughts, emotions, reactions,*** and ***actions.***

2. ***Question:*** constantly question any unbalanced ***thoughts, emotions, reactions,*** and ***actions, to see what belief system is fueling them?***

3. ***Self-honesty***: be *really, really, honest about what is the motivation behind* your ***thoughts, emotions, actions,*** and ***reactions.***

4. ***Choice: choose*** how ***you react*** (via the authentic you not the Ego you) to ***everything*** in your life.

Is what you see in your life mirror a challenge or opportunity?

Inauthentic inherited belief systems that have become your reality are what you see reflected in your life mirror, as your life challenges.

To get you on the road to connecting with your authentic self, let's look at various expressions such as, 'every challenge is a blessing' and 'challenge is an opportunity for personal growth'. I never really found an outside explanation that helped me fully understand this, and when in the middle of some of my early personal 'challenges'; I found these statements highly insensitive and irritating.

So here is my version. I hope it helps, and as always, I share nothing I have not personally experienced or witnessed in others.

Living our human based existence, we have come to view life, generally, from a point of hardship, stress, lack and suffering.

Working really hard, rushing, worry, fear and stress, is ingrained in us, and to depart from these automatic beliefs can be scary, because what else is there?

The fact that we view a challenge or trauma from a point of suffering continues to keep us very nicely where we are. It reinforces our human belief systems, and keeps them firmly in place.

Imagine viewing a challenge as an opportunity to get to know yourself better, and improve your life.

I know, it seems to go against everything that we regard as sensible, yet we accept it as quite sensible to try and achieve happiness through our life model of: over work, striving, struggle, competitiveness, lack of self-care, and stress.

This is certainly not a sensible approach. But it has become our collective, unconscious response to society's expectations of us.

So, how do we bring about sensible life balance and change, through challenges?

Firstly, as you know energy makes up our world and is ***only potential*** until we place our expectations and focus on it. Therefore, challenges (manifestations of our beliefs and experiences), can be the best tool to discover where we have beliefs that do not belong to us, and need transforming.

We have two ways of looking at life's challenges: either through conscious awareness, consciously creating our thoughts and reactions to produce new situations, or we can meet challenges, unconsciously, as victims, using our repetitive reactions because that's what we have always done.

Our challenges are not random; we have a limited human belief system that produces an expectation, which manifests into a situation or challenge. We create our reality by instructing energy to form according to our expectations of life.

Your life circumstances are the mirror into your deepest emotions and expectations. If your current reality is unfulfilling, unhappy, fearful, or contains challenges right now, this is the exact place to begin your transformational process.

My physical and mental illnesses were the challenges that helped me to start the process of change and transformation. At the time, I would have questioned anyone who could dare to suggest I 'chose' to be ill. But looking back I did choose and manifest those illnesses; without them I would not be here today. My illnesses were what I needed to see beyond my repetitive behaviour, they got my attention due to the clear message of "step up and listen, or leave".

Further along my transformational process I faced many more 'challenges'.

For anyone, the death of a loved one is one of the most challenging. When I was faced with this situation, the suggestion that I would 'benefit' from such an emotionally complex life event, I would have found completely insensitive and harsh. But I grew in unimaginable ways through the death of my dearest Dad.

My Dad was my hero, the love of my life, my inspiration and I watched him die in the most horrendous of circumstances, and during the last weeks of his life, due to others mistakes, he suffered in a way no one should ever have to, and I witnessed almost every moment.

When he passed, I was numb, not able to process what had happened. Despite all the different emotions running riot inside me, I knew I had to move into the grieving process with awareness, or things could go very wrong.

The healing process took time, but I questioned everyday my thoughts, emotions, and where I was taking myself with the reactions I was choosing. I always held onto the fact that I know there is a reason for everything, and there is always (eventually) something positive to move into from a perceived challenge, and most importantly, I was not a victim; I had included this in my life experience for a reason!

There were many days when all I could do was draw on raw courage and complete trust that the universe and my Primary Self had my back. I had most certainly arrived at another choice point in my life, do I blame the world for making the last weeks with my Dad unbearable? Do I become angry and bitter and fuel my Ego with a lifelong feast of negativity and blame?

I knew through experience, by making the choice to hold anger, blame, and hurt inside, these emotions would control my life forever, and most likely eventually make me ill. I knew if I allowed my thoughts to go into overdrive, reliving the trauma that I saw, I would literally drive myself mad.

My life, and the life of my family would change forever, and not for the better.

My choice? Yes, even at that time of emotional upheaval; I had a choice. I knew my choices had to come from a place of conscious awareness, a place of love, my choices had to come from my heart, not my Ego.

So, I made my choice from a point of love for myself and love for my Dad. I chose to focus on all the great times I had with my Dad, to focus my energy and thoughts on complete gratitude that I even had the chance to have such a wonderful Dad. My choice was to focus on the positive things my Dad had the opportunity to experience in his life.

My focus was not to shut out what happened, but to focus and direct my energy on the fact that what happened over the time my Dad spent suffering, was only a small part of his life.

My choice was to give thanks for his life, and having him in my life. That was my decision when I reached ***my choice point***.

From the choices I made I learnt so much about myself; I observed a great deal about life on many levels, and learnt a great deal about the human perceptions and experience of death.

But, the biggest gift I received from my Dad was to be able to learn how to forgive and trust; forgive unconditionally, and trust without waiver. As many of you may know our choices around forgiveness have the ability to destroy us, or offer us unimaginable freedom. I ***chose*** the latter. This choice changed my reality forever.

Because of my choices, I learnt new perspectives on many levels, achieving these new perspectives through Awareness, Questioning, Self-Honesty, and Choice. By using this process I was able to see a much bigger picture than just the 'incident'.

I guided myself to a better outcome.

The ultimate truth is; anything that is a negative heavy emotion or reaction does not belong to you. It is a part of you that has been created as a defence mechanism in order to protect the inauthentic weakened version of you that is trying to survive without its true identity.

As conscious, authentic energy beings, our ultimate programming is Love, Love for ourselves, Love for each other, and Love for all the natural world.

I don't just mean the kissy kissy love (although that is lovely too), I am talking all-powerful, deeply respectful, deeply reverent, and the original ultimate powerhouse of Love that is our authentic self.

Anything outside of this original state of being, produced by the weakened, diluted version of yourself, can bring about challenges that help you to break the unhealthy patterns of the past.

These 'challenges' can heal you from the past and bring who you authentically are to life. As you embark on this process, you will begin to not only remember your creator power, you will become it.

You will begin to create a reality that no longer reflects your past and you can enjoy life, standing in your power as a creator and live according to your purpose for being here.

The life 'challenges' I have shared with you enabled me to release the specific parts of me that were not authentic. I will never be faced with life 'challenges' that offer me the opportunity to release those specific emotions again.

I have been there, faced painful personal truths, changed my energy, and I will never need to experience it again. The unreal 'man'-ufactured human emotions that were brought to my attention by these challenges no longer have a home in my reality.

I have found beautiful parts of me that were hidden under generations of complex human emotions. The emotions and energy that now reside where the old stuff was, is forgiveness, courage, trust in the process of life, and unconditional love.

I thank my Dad, who is with me every day, helping me write, and supporting my family, for allowing me to be with him for what was not just an opportunity for me to grow but an opportunity for him to release before he stepped out of his physical body, and flew!

As a side note, I regularly talk about and know that everything is perfect in every moment. Well, it came as no surprise to me that I had no enthusiasm or drive to write this part of the chapter when I had scheduled the time in. The day I did write this part coincided with the exact anniversary date of my Dad's death. How is that for synchronicity?

And me being me, never missing an opportunity to ***question*** and discover, I realised I had been given the gift of putting my experience down on paper, on the date of my dad's death as an opportunity to see if I still had any attachment to what I experienced, or had I really released and moved on? I had a good delve around and I am happy to report, I could write every word without attachment, and with deep gratitude and love.

Anyway, back to the learning. These two examples of my challenges highlight the way you can process an experience and the beliefs you then form as a consequence. How you process any experience becomes the basis of what creates your reality.

Your reality is mostly based on the reactions you have, that are unhelpfully influenced by the collective belief systems of society, which are mainly governed by Ego and past programming.

The challenges I have just described are the bigger events but also be aware of the smaller challenges, the type that drip, drip, into your life. The smaller, more mundane boring stuff, not necessarily the big attention-grabbing ones, but the niggling problems or dissatisfactions. These smaller 'challenges' may not need such deep excavation, but they are still as important in the long run.

All challenges, big or small are opportunities to remove the ***pieces of your past from your present***, and replace them with the authentic pieces of yourself.

Don't Wait Assignment

This can be a bit of a challenging chapter because it breaks down the untruths of the life you are experiencing and offers something very different than the guidelines you have been programmed to operate by. That can sometimes bring up some resistance because this new knowledge on the one hand represents such freedom, but it also means change, and the Ego doesn't like change, it prefers to keep things just as they are, so it can keep you just where you are, with set limitations… forever.

But we aren't here to keep you where you are, we aren't here to wait for the rest of the world to get better, we are her to assist you to fly to great knew heights of experience, fulfilment, and happiness.

The 4 steps I mentioned earlier in the chapter are the steps that WILL absolutely assist you at every turn, corner, emotion, and challenge of your daily life. Initially it is a process that takes a bit of thought and a bit of concentration, BUT as it becomes automatic it means you can decode your challenges, unhelpful habits and the beliefs that are creating your experiences into something that makes far more sense, holds far more meaning, and then creates the magical life you desire, not the life you have been programmed to live.

So, make the 4-step process in this chapter the top priority in your life, everyday:

1. Awareness
2. Question
3. Self-honesty
4. Choice

I would recommend you writing the full detail of each point from this chapter in your journal, and then put reminders in place to keep them in the forefront of your mind (they work really well as a screen saver ☺), until they become automatic, because with a little investment they will.

These 4 steps are the key to freeing yourself from the old generational programming and moving into a bright expansive future.

Chapter 16

Stand Tall And Take A Look In Your Mirror

Changing the Reflection

Many, many people stick with mundane or difficult life situations such as relationships, work or health challenges, day after day rather than face change, due to fear.

If you want to change something in your life, but are scared and fearful, the best way to achieve the change you want, is to face it head on, while embracing the trust and freedom your new understanding of challenges gives you.

When you face something head on it loses its grip, loses its power, the fear disappears, and you never face that unhappiness again.

Let me further explain how the universe, the people in your life, and your Primary Self are trying to reach you, and help you become you again.

Life challenges that appear are energy manifestations from your programmed beliefs. These challenges present you with the situations/

challenges you need to reconnect with yourself, and recognise you are going against what is right for you.

However, an error has occurred in translating the messages. We have translated the information into something that fits our current materialist worldview.

The challenges presented to us, we perceive as negative, because we are using our materialistic human translator, which will always see the negative, because that is what keeps us firmly rooted in our learnt behaviour patterns of fear and insignificance.

Viewing life this way leaves us feeling like victims of random events, out of control and at the mercy of an unpredictable life; you now know that this is certainly not the case.

In my experience, every challenge has a motivation of love behind it. It has your personal conscious energy behind it and here is why.

How do we move on from and release the negative emotions and behaviour patterns we have inherited over the generations? By having them pointed out to us, via the reflection of your life.

Seems crazy that you would need these emotional behaviour patterns pointed out to you, but often they are so ingrained, or so automatic, you don't even realise they are there. Alternatively, you recognise their presence, but would rather not see them.

So, firstly you need to recognise, face, or be nudged towards that which is not you, but has become you.

With a life challenge, either mild or serious, comes the opportunity for you to ***discover what does not belong to you,*** and needs to be transformed.

Your challenge will create within you the exact emotions, learnt behaviour or resistance you need to clear.

If you have some anger within, your life challenge will reflect that right back at you, with a situation or situations that makes you mildly, or very angry.

If you have witnessed dysfunctional relationships as a child, and carry beliefs, due to memories/emotional residue, that relationships are dysfunctional, you may find you are presented with dysfunctional relationship situations, which bring the original emotions to the surface to heal.

If you were brought up to believe you look after everyone else first before yourself, you may be presented with a health challenge that encourages self-care and self-love.

If you were bullied at school and put those memories away somewhere inside, you may be presented with a very dominant bully in your adult life, to bring the same emotions up to heal.

If you believe that life is a struggle, and your belief in lack is stronger than your belief in abundance, you may experience financial issues.

A life challenge is not some random event. It is precise. Challenges are there to push your buttons, so you know exactly what ingrained behaviour patterns, and beliefs of others, need to be transformed.

The challenge is only the facilitator to discovering a bigger picture; it is never solely about the details of the challenge.

The authentic you, knows exactly what you need to release, and brings it to you on a plate.

In my experience, we humans do not like change, because we view change as loss, which we fear. We will often keep repeating negative behaviour over and over rather than step up and transform.

I have done exactly that, everything that was not working in my life, I initially complained about and blamed on anything, and everyone. I believed I was a victim of life and so became just that.

What I really needed was courage. Courage to have self-honesty, to look into myself, and be really honest about what was, and was not working.

I needed to face my negative emotions, fear, and insecurities as they arose, with self-honesty and understand why I felt the need to react in a certain way.

Often we will sidestep ourselves, even up to the moment of death, before we are really honest, and then pass over with regrets.

That is what life's challenges can offer you, opportunity and choice.

Opportunity to choose your old, outdated, hand me down, emotional reactions or choose your original 'divine' programming.

If I had known this, in the early days, during the times I perceived as 'tough' and 'traumatic', I would have understood these events were just a way of achieving a better me, a better life and freedom from miscreated emotional behaviour. I would have realised I am the creator of my life, and have everything within me to transform challenge through choice.

My perceived challenges have shaped me, helped me to uncover information, gifts, and a life I would never have thought possible.

My challenges have allowed me to become my authentic self with unlimited possibilities (I am writing a book for goodness sake, I never imagined that as a possibility)!

Life's perceived challenges enable you to find the positive by presenting you with the opposite.

Whatever emotional/reactive button is being pressed, you need to recognise, and nurture new authentic qualities in yourself.

It is very, very, rare we ever volunteer to really, honestly review ourselves, and our lives. We carry on living life disconnected from our true potential, until something or someone comes into our life, and gives us a nudge.

Maybe now is your time to stand tall, and take a look in your mirror?

Now, let's take a moment to refresh our memory.

As human beings, we have turned ourselves into insignificant beings. We have blocked ourselves off from the guidance and energy of our Primary Self, and forgotten our place in the much bigger picture of Universal Society.

While living our exclusively human existence, we have over time, created highly emotional complex behaviours to try and satisfy our need for identity, significance, and love.

These survival emotions have been hard wired (remember the pathways created in our brain) over generations, and become who we think we are. However, transformation is completely possible.

We have discussed 'challenges' and I want to make sure you are aware of how we define challenges.

A 'challenge' can be on an emotionally reactive level, anything from a small negative reaction to a full-on meltdown, and all the emotions that can include. Or a 'challenge' can be what appears to come from external events such as losing a job, illness, and other life events.

A 'challenge' is anything at all that creates a reaction within you that is not a balanced one!

I want to keep this information as simple as possible, because it does not need to be complicated in order for you to see what is already within you.

How do you put into practice moving into your authentic self and best life?

By remembering these next two sentences, at all times, every day, every moment.

Any thought/feeling/emotion *that is not creating balance within you is* ***not your authentic self.***

Any reaction *you have, that is not balanced,*
is ***not your authentic self.***

(NB. Any reaction that is out of balance can include positive reactions too)

These two points are true because the only time we feel 'challenged' to negatively react, defend ourselves, or feel emotionally unbalanced, is when we react to something we feel is a threat to us.

But what we see as a threat is based on our need to defend our insignificance, and defend the insecurities that we have created for ourselves, through our materialistic existence.

We have processed these perceived threats through the lens of others life experiences, and generations of emotional programming. We have not processed these perceived threats through the lens of our authentic selves.

When you see through the lens of your authentic self, there can be ***no threat***. Because the authentic you knows who you are. You have no insecurities to defend, because ***YOU ARE already identity, significance, and love.***

These perceived threats ***only become real*** because we ***choose to give our energy and focus to our insecurities, and not look at the message behind the challenge.***

When you are consciously aware of your reactions and feelings, you are tuned into yourself completely. You are listening for the clues that you are giving yourself, clues to what is part of you, and what is not.

We as human beings have created our miscreation's. These miscreated thoughts, emotions, and behaviours are who you have become.

If you continue to recreate them, by living your life unconsciously, without thought or awareness, nothing will change.

The good news is, things are changing. You are not alone; many are looking for change, for proof of a better life and world. There is literally mass dissatisfaction, creating mass 'awakening' to new thinking, a new way, and a new future.

Being consciously aware of a fresh, new way to deal with challenges, can fast track you to clearing all that does not belong to you, and help you to be the best version of you.

You are constantly guiding yourself towards perfect life situations. Remember this is you talking to you; you are not a victim of circumstance.

Please do stop and listen to these challenges because they are messages, they are clues created by you, that all is not balanced within your inner world.

My work and personal experience has taught me that where there is imbalance in your experience of life or imbalance within your physical body, *there are current or past-unaddressed memories/ emotions or negative learnt behaviour,* and consequently you are not honouring yourself.

Unbalanced, negative emotions carry a heavy, dense vibration that literally, over time, clogs the flow of your life force. Every emotion (which is an energy vibration) forms matter and creates a physical chemical reaction in the body.

You will have experienced this through physical symptoms, which is energy conforming to your instruction to form matter.

For example, the feeling of butterflies in your tummy when you are nervous. In this instance, a thought instructs energy to form matter, producing a chemical reaction, which produces a physical reaction/feeling of nervousness. It started as a thought but manifested as a chemical and physical reaction.

Unbalanced thoughts have an impact not only by instructing matter to give you your life experiences, but also by forming matter to influence your physical body.

Some of the signs you may experience as challenges when not living as your authentic self can include:

- Emotional/mental symptoms such as: feelings of unrest, boredom, anxiety, lack of enthusiasm, insecurities, lack of self-confidence, mood changes, anxiety, depression, and any emotion that leaves you feeling regularly unbalanced.

- Any need to regularly change your experience of life, such as through alcohol, drugs, sleeping a lot, gossiping, excessive exercise, watching lots of TV, over or under eating, creating drama in your life, focusing on others drama, the need to constantly control others or your environment, and a need to constantly achieve.

- Life experience symptoms may include: difficult relationships with friends/colleagues/family, financial problems, work issues, and any other negative events or life situations.

- Physical symptoms may include: digestive issues, tiredness, colds, ongoing niggling ailments, and health challenges in the form of illness and dis-ease.

When your body is not functioning efficiently or life is not running smoothly, there is a reason.

This is the point when you need to look and listen, because you are trying to communicate with yourself, via your physical body or life situation. A nudge to help you realise, that on some level all is not well, and you are not being honest with yourself and you are not living authentically.

If you do not hear the nudges of your True Self long term, this may go one of two ways.

Firstly, you may continue to live as you have always done.

Never quite reaching your potential, having sporadic niggling health issues and perhaps having a need to continue to change your experience of life, through your preferred method. Ultimately, you continue to live a life that is familiar, but in moments of real self- honesty, you know, you are unfulfilled.

The second option might be: in comes the bigger challenge. Often more attention grabbing, physical or mental health challenges, or more attention-grabbing life situations.

How you deal with all your perceived challenges, depends on your ability to communicate with yourself, give yourself valuable airtime, and most important of all, your ability for self-honesty.

By choosing a higher thought process (see the four points on page 102), and using honest self-talk, you will change your experience of any perceived challenge, for the better.

The key here is, when presented with a challenge, see it for what it is, an opportunity to release an aspect of you that is not authentic, something you no longer need or want.

At this point, just be aware of the emotion/event, but ***do not*** become it.

Remember, you are watching a movie, not playing a part within it. Regardless of how gripping it is, it's external to you, but may connect to old scenes from your own life.

For me personally, when it comes to challenges, I question myself deeply. What buttons are being pressed? What insecurities/fears are being highlighted? Why do I feel the need to react? What is it I am missing here?

I question until I find my ***honest*** answer. Not an answer that bolsters my Ego but the answer that exposes my weakness and insecurity, because that is where truth lies.

It's an uncomfortable process facing your weakness, but liberating beyond words when you recognise, release and replace the old goo that really isn't you.

When facing a challenge: Acknowledge it, but DO NOT become it, the more airtime you give any negative or fearful thoughts, the stronger the energy of the emotion/event becomes, by giving it your full attention means you are re fueling it.

Be completely aware of your reactions in the moment and long term, and choose higher thoughts, acknowledge your choice point and utilise it. Choose how much power and influence you give to your specific thoughts and feelings.

Whether you are dealing with an in the moment challenge (e.g. someone's opinions or judgements press your buttons) or longer- term challenge (e.g. job insecurity or problems within the family), you always have a choice in how you react, however difficult you perceive a situation you can choose a higher, more positive, and productive thought or an ego-based victim reaction.

Remember, the reaction or emotion you choose is energy, and will form matter. This is exactly the moments where your reality, your life experience is created.

Allow negative, reactive, or emotional energy, whenever and however often it arises, to move through you, and away. You can be aware of it but do not give your focus and energy to it; it is past programming and does not belong to you. The negative energy of the event will transform itself through your awareness and intention to release.

Also be ***very aware*** of **Secondary Emotions** (Ego again). These are the emotions that you create in your mind that distract you from the original feeling, and create a much more complicated and unnecessarily dramatic scenario.

For example, if you are feeling really tired, rather than just holding awareness of your tiredness. Allowing it to communicate so you can positively soften your actions to support yourself, and create a solution to this **one** issue. We (Ego) creates secondary emotions.

In this instance we **start with feeling over tired** and then we complicate things with unnecessary secondary emotions that include: all the reasons why we are so tired, how much more we still have to do today, tomorrow, this week, who in our life hasn't helped us enough, how cross we are about that, and everyone expects us to do everything!

We have probably had arguments with people in our mind and decided we just have to soldier on regardless, because no one will bother to help us anyway. Sound familiar?

With this elaborate thought process, we move ourselves completely away from the simplicity of dealing with the feeling of being over tired, to accessorising this feeling with additional unhelpful emotions.

We successfully distract our self from our self and make finding a solution and implementing it impossible, because we don't even know what the real problem is anymore.

We create secondary emotions all the time, to commentate on many different situations.

Being aware of, and only act on the original emotion or feeling, allow yourself to find an uncomplicated solution, without any added drama and fully support yourself.

If at any time, for whatever reason, it is not possible to access higher thoughts and see the bigger picture in the moment, engage in something else and move your thoughts to something unrelated that helps you feel calm, peaceful, and happy.

This is not avoidance, but a simple way to detach from reacting to the present moment experience in an unhelpful way. You can, if necessary, come back to holding the intention to release and heal the situation when you feel more balanced.

With this awareness, your ability to move through these moments is powerful. But it is imperative to remember each and every time that, ***you are facing a point of choice,*** you choose the old negative reactions, or create new honest positive reactions.

Each time you remember, in those moments of fear and challenge, that you are being presented with an opportunity from yourself, from the conscious you, you are instantly released from fear, and the feeling of being a victim and out of control.

You are teaching yourself how to effectively release fear and resistance when it arises. Where you have resistance, you have attachment, where you have attachment you have fear, fear of loss, fear of change. However ugly the old stuff is, it is familiar, and Ego will cause great resistance to the new.

This simple process is well worth memorising and putting in place to assist you through the process of transformation (challenges):

1. In your mind visualise and create yourself an observation platform. A simple, comfortable, safe place where you stand in your power as the creative, wise being that you are.

2. From this platform you can view situations from a place of detachment, as an onlooker. Your observation point will be an invaluable bit of kit to support you in easily releasing all that is not you. Make sure it is available at all times

3. As an unbalanced emotion/reaction occurs simply observe it from your platform. Observe the emotion but do not become it, do not move into it, just be an observer of it.

4. By observing the emotion/reaction you do not become it, you simply just allow it to surface, and then move on through.

5. Fill the space of unbalanced reaction with the authentic you, conscious directed thoughts/reactions, the opposite of what you are releasing.

6. When your focus then moves to the shiny new authentic emotion, that is where your energy goes and creates your reality, your new reality.

7. Be aware you may need to use this process only once to move out the old stuff, and at other times it may take a few more go's before the deeper held beliefs move on. Either way, it's all good.

8. Be proud of yourself and be kind to yourself.

This transformation thing can be challenging, frustrating, and at times all consuming, but these challenging periods enable us to go deeper than we are able to when our minds are focused on the usual distractions of everyday life.

The deeper we go, and the more truth we have the courage to recover, the higher we get to fly when we come out the other side and fly you will!

Also remember, there is no such thing as getting it wrong in life, you do the best you can with where you are, and what you have available at the time.

If a challenge presents itself, and you slip back into amnesia and forget your power, you are simply offered another opportunity, a '***next time***' to remember your power as a creative being (think repetitive life situations, basically it happens again), and you present yourself, lovingly with another opportunity.

As you are reading this book, chances are you are ready to change. On some level you have made the decision to start the process of transforming your life. You no longer believe you are living authentically, and you know there is something more. You may not have any idea what that 'more' is but there is something inside you that is restless.

At this point you begin sending out a new energy instruction, even on the most subtle thought process, you create. Just as I described earlier, the moment I sat on my bed knowing I had to do something, wasn't sure what, or where it would take me, but I knew there had to be something.

When you do step up, the challenges (clearing) can speed up, this is nothing to be fearful of, but important to be aware of. It is character building (literally), you learn to trust deeply and by living consciously, your new beliefs become authentic, and well and truly anchored as your shiny new reality.

At the point I made my decision to move forward, what I needed 'appeared' in my life, and my new thoughts created new instructions that began to manifest. This produced 'challenges' that exposed programmed behaviours, and beliefs about myself and the world.

These 'challenges' cleared out the outdated stuff that belonged to others, my miscreated emotional reactions, and the authentic me, began to emerge from under the goo.

What also arrived in my life were the exact opportunities, people and circumstances to assist my desire for change, all created by my thoughts manifesting into form, and some help from the universal community.

So, you choose when the time is right to step up, but do it sooner rather than later.

The authentic you is waiting to emerge, create, and become all you have ever dreamed of. Which, incidentally is far more than you could ever imagine is possible, through your human mind.

Life experience is not created by external forces, or situations, life experience is created from within you.

Remember, everything you wish to experience in the physical world cannot be created from the physical world; your life experiences are created by the reactive choices you make from within.

(i.e. thoughts, decisions, and emotions).

Every one of your life experiences is created in the moment, within your internal world. How you react will be dependent on your own personal belief systems. This is why we all have different experiences of the same life events.

Don't Wait Assignment

The absolute point of this chapter is for you to take away and live the following:

In any situation, how you choose to direct your thoughts, your energy, and your focus, will be how you choose the outcome.

The reactions and emotions you choose, create your reality, you are the creator of your life, and your reality.

You choose what your reality is, because energy conforms to your beliefs to form matter, your human experience is purely a reflection of your internal world.

Only what you choose becomes real. You have the gift of free thought, free will, and conscious creation........ now use it wisely!

Chapter 17

Health, Dis-ease And Loving You

Could you love yourself more?

Simple answer; is almost certainly yes.

A natural part of your self-discovery is to relearn Self Care, and Self Love. Self-Care and Self Love appears to be one of the biggest challenges we face personally and globally.

It is my belief, that this is a reflection of how insignificant we feel within ourselves, because we exist as part of a society that recognises materialistic and financial achievements as a measure of us as human beings.

Society gives recognition, praise, approval, acceptance, and love to a false materialistic identity, the very same identity we then accept as ourselves.

We are measured by our external achievements, and have lost appreciation and gratitude for ourselves as a whole. We can never truly love something that is false, and this is where the stumbling block occurs.

To love ourselves unconditionally for the perfect beings that we are, and to fully appreciate and respect ourselves, we need to lose the false self with which we judge ourselves and on which we are judged.

Real Self Love, Self-Acceptance, and Self-Respect is a very difficult thing for us to achieve because we see ourselves as solely human, and carry with us all the distorted beliefs we have been given about ourselves, and our world.

These beliefs are far removed from the beauty that each one of us actually is, and therefore **we struggle to love that which is not truth.**

This is why we have an epidemic of self-neglect, whether it be neglect through substance use, diet, exercise, alcohol, smoking, unbalanced behaviour/thoughts, or any other area of self-care. If we grasped the utter magnitude of who we are, and the miracle of our physical and eternal existence, we would never ever treat ourselves with anything other than love and respect.

Fundamentally, our lack of self-love is created, yet again, by our loss of identity. We are trying to love other people's stuff that has become who we are, and *we can't ever fully love that which is not authentic.*

This issue is at the crux of our health and wellbeing while in human form, understanding who we are creates reverence, respect, and love. This is then reflected in our self-care. Mental and physical health often clearly reflect the state of our internal world.

Your human body is the miracle that enables you to experience human life. Its absolute magnificence is so intricately and precisely designed, that science is a million miles away from uncovering and understanding all its wonder.

Your human body carries you through every moment of your life experience. Bring to mind a momentous time in your life, a great happiness, a milestone, an incredible life experience. Have you ever thought, that throughout that experience your body was giving you life, enabling you to feel, touch, smell, and embrace every second; supporting you in every moment?

Your body does this without question, unconditionally, every day you are alive. Your body loves you unconditionally, and we take this for granted (due to lack of understanding).

Your body wants to be well, it wants to heal, your body is pre-programmed to heal and thrive, but it needs you to provide the environment.

Your body will try its best to keep you in balance despite what you put in it. Your body will forgive you unconditionally for the barrage of chemical reactions that flow through your bloodstream, because of your emotional state.

How do you respect and nurture your body? How do you show your body gratitude for its unrelenting work every day of your life?

During your lifetime as a human being, *nothing* gives to you in the same way as your body does; it will carry you through *every* moment of your life until the day you die.

When I grasped the magnitude of this, I felt, and still do every day, incredibly humbled and grateful. I realised this was not about noticing my body for how fat or thin it is. This is not about noticing the superficial stuff.

This is about finally becoming aware that, You (insert your name here) have in your care, one of the most incredible 'machines' ever created! You (insert your name here) are in charge of something so complex it cannot be replicated.

Without the blessing of a human body, you and I would not have the opportunity of living life.

I give thanks for that every day.

The Bigger Questions About Health and Wellness

Despite being blessed with the most incredible 'machine' on the planet, how have we ended up feeling so out of control of our bodies and our own health? Why is dis-ease so prevalent and why are we living in fear of illness?

You know it's simple really, and yet we can't 'see' it. We are in fear of illness, are given confusing and often conflicting advice on how to stay well, and bombarded with media telling us how much illness is out there, just waiting to pounce on us.

Well, I want you to stop living in fear. I want to give you some other choices other than fear.

Here are my thoughts on some of the reasons we are becoming unwell, my thoughts on the process of manifesting illness, and some observations about how we view dis-ease, collectively and as individuals.

This information is based on my years of personal and client-based experience.

Back to the now familiar, and fundamental, basis of everything.

We have created our insignificance; we have forgotten who we are, we have forgotten our creative power, and have forgotten our ability to communicate with ourselves. It's the same cause at the root of everything!

We have lost trust in ourselves because of our created insignificance, and have handed our health, and wellbeing, over to others.

Lack of trust in ourselves has been further reinforced over time by how the physical body is viewed from a point of medical science. The scientific method reduces us, and the natural world to a mathematic equation. Any healthcare practices gained through personal experience are treated as anecdotal, totally disregarding and disconnecting us from our own personal wisdom.

Disconnection from ourselves, living with the emotional complexities of our human existence, the belief that we are mathematical equations, that our environment and our experience and knowledge of ourselves are considered insignificant, all result in a very powerful combination that creates your disempowerment and fear.

Despite all this disempowering information, what you need to remember at all times is that the human body is designed, and programmed to stay physically, and mentally healthy. Your body will do everything it can to keep you well, heal your ailments, illnesses, and accidents.

Every day you can read and hear statistics, articles, and media reports about our current state of health. Obesity, serious dis- eases, mental illness are under constant debate, and if we believe the statistics it all seems hopeless.

I am not disregarding the fact that there are not big issues with physical and mental health, but what I want to do is give you another angle, another viewpoint.

I believe that our perceived insignificance, self-doubt, lack of selfself-care, lack of selfself-love, disconnection from our bodies, and our inner voice, are all powerful examples of why **dis-ease** appears to be manifesting itself so abundantly in society.

I want you to stop living in fear, I want you to have other empowering perspectives that you can move forward with.

So, let's look at how to further empower your miracle self, and your miracle 'machine'!

Learnt behaviour vs. Inherited illness

Throughout this chapter my aim is to get you thinking from a different angle and exploring what you 'feel' when reading new information and experiencing different perspectives on health and wellbeing. As always, be aware of what 'feels' right, don't just think it through.

Inherited illness is an area of health and wellness that is a real concern to many. It can create fear because of the perceived 'unknown' outcome of an inherited dis-ease on our own health. Many live with the health worry that members of their family have been 'struck' by a *dis-ease,* creating the thought process of "is it just a matter of time for me"?

In order to look in more detail, you need some information to build on, to help you understand a little of the process of health and dis-ease.

Most of you have probably encountered or heard reference to DNA relating to the function of our bodies. DNA, is the instruction manual on how to build living things.

DNA is made up of genes. Genes provide the blueprint for the design of the human body and how it develops.

The word Genome is a combination of the word Gene and Chromosome, and refers to the genetic information of an organism.

Genes **do not** make decisions about what they do, or whether they are turned on or turned off.

The DNA in our body is wrapped around proteins called Histones. Both the DNA and Histones are covered in chemical tags. This second layer of structure is called the Epigenome.

The Epigenome affects the physical structure of the genes, it tightly wraps inactive genes to make them unreadable and it relaxes active genes, making them easily accessible. The Epigenome is a multitude of chemical compounds that can tell a genome what to do.

Changes in the Epigenome can switch on or off genes involved in cell growth or immune response, and affect how genes are expressed and used.

The Epigenome is covered in chemical tags; think of these tags as post-it notes that highlight particular genes with information about whether they should be switched on or off.

The Gene follows instructions that are not in the genome, they are in the Epigenome. The chemical compounds of the Epigenome tell the Gene what to do, and these chemical compounds are influenced by ***our internal and external environment.***

Alterations to the DNA are made in response to your ***environment,*** which includes your ***surroundings, experiences, diet*** and ***personal behaviour.***

Your Epigenome is flexible and Epigenetic Tags react to signals from your internal environment, and the outside world.

What this indicates is your Epigenetic markers are flexible and can be rewritten, which means that you can modify the instructions your genes receive, ***through the creation of your external and internal environment.***

Environmental factors reach and talk to the Epigenome through cell signalling. Some signals are direct; the foods we eat are broken down and circulate through the body. Some signals are indirect; stress, negative thoughts, and emotions can trigger an array of signals that move from cell to cell through the release of brain chemicals and hormones. The Epigenome will then issue instructions to the DNA, according to the environmental messages it receives.

Environmental signals such as diet, stress, thoughts/emotions, and environmental toxins, can trigger changes, via the Epigenome, in gene expression!

Our DNA is widely regarded as the instruction book for the human body, but genes themselves need instructions for what to do. The Epigenome activates these instructions like a complex software code, capable of inducing DNA hardware to manufacture an impressive variety of proteins, and cell types.

More and more researchers are finding that a dietary tweak, exposure to a toxin, and even a dose of nurturing from a loved one can tweak the Epigenome, and thereby alter the software of our genes.

We commonly accept the notion that through our DNA we are destined to have particular dis-eases. Your gene's predetermining your fate has become one of society's created truths.

Through the study of Epigenetics, that notion is at last proving outdated. Epigenetics is proving we do have some control over our genetic legacy. Our physical body reacts to our internal and external environment.

Our internal and external environment is only potential until we place our focus on it, then it becomes our reality, and that reality affects us physically, it contributes to physical changes in our body.

Our belief systems govern what we manifest, both internally and externally, and contribute to creating our health.

Epigenetics is helping us understand that we have options and choices when it comes to our health.

It's not the 'inherited' dis-ease that follows a person around waiting to pounce. It is the environment that is reproduced within a person that

favours the development of a particular dis-ease via the learnt behaviour of previous generations.

Learnt behaviour passed down the generations produces the environment that favours a particular dis-ease, enabling it to develop. The learnt behaviour produces repetitive thoughts, emotions, and judgements of the world that affect our body chemistry, that impact our Epigenetics, that send signals to instruct our genes, to turn on or turn off.

Inherited 'dis-ease', when approached from this viewpoint, is a result of learnt behaviour, passed down through the generations, that produces the specific environment for your 'specific inherited' dis-ease to manifest.

It is not only the thoughts and emotional responses that can produce physical changes, but also the way in which the learnt behaviour impacts our attitude and actions towards how we look after ourselves, for example through diet and lifestyle.

Throughout the past twenty years working on my own personal development and working with my clients, I discovered there was a specific link between particular behaviours and emotions, and how they have an effect on specific areas of the body. What this means is that specific emotions, produce specific chemical responses within the body, and these particular chemical changes affect a particular area/organ of the body.

To clarify, from an energy perspective; an emotion carries a specific energy vibration that directly affects the energy vibration of a particular organ or area in the body, changing its healthy vibrational frequency, producing physical changes in how the body expresses itself physically.

For instance, my experience working with clients who have breast problems, usually coincides with personality traits and emotions relating to giving, nurturing, nourishing, and mothering everyone else, but these clients often have great difficulty in practicing self-nourishment, self-love, and self-care for themselves.

Health issues arising in the reproductive area, I have found, most often relate to how in control we feel of our external environment, concerns in areas such money, and relationships. This area represents our need to have some control over the physical dynamics of our external environment.

I have often found, high blood pressure usually relates back to an emotional problem that has not been solved. Usually a long-standing emotional problem or trauma that has never been resolved.

Areas of imbalance in the throat area, usually relate back to a person having a 'voice'. Expressing themselves through their voice, and also their voice and opinions being heard, and most importantly valued. It can also reflect a person's inability to express themselves and emotions (energy) get 'stuck in their throat'.

As always, when we take this information back to basics, every thought emotion and behaviour carries an energy vibration that manifests into physical form within the body. Your thoughts and emotions will determine whether the vibration is one that is supportive or unsupportive of your physical health.

You see, the idea that you are destined to the fate of an inherited illness is a conclusion reached by just looking at the physical manifestation of dis-ease. It does not take into consideration the environmental instructions required for the relevant DNA to be switched on or off, in my experience these instructions come from repetitive learnt behaviour traits, which create chemical reactions within the body. It is the learnt beliefs and consequent learnt behaviour patterns that are carried down the generations, not a random dis-ease that just happens to appear in a family. It is all about the environment, the environment we manifest in our physical body, via our learnt behaviour.

Based on this information, I would recommend, from this moment, you are never without a physical symptom and emotional reference guidebook, such as "You Can Heal Your Life" by Louise Hay. This will encourage you to work with and understand your body.

Whether it be a passing health niggle, an illness or dis-ease, you can cross reference the problem with the corresponding emotion/ behaviour traits and become a detective into what event, emotion, or external situation your body is responding to. This will assist you with clear direction as to what is balanced in your life and gives you an opportunity to rebalance the areas causing your body to respond.

You will never have better clues than the ones from your own body to guide you to health, and emotional balance. All you have to do is listen consciously, and you remove the fear of illness, and empower yourself towards health.

Always remember your body is programmed to serve your human experience, and if you have health issues it is your body trying to get your attention, it is your body communicating with you.

When you work with this information, you understand that in every moment, with each thought, feeling and choice you make, ***you are engineering your own health***, via your Epigenome.

You don't have to be just a victim to inherited illness, you now know you have health choices, through choosing different, conscious thoughts and behaviour.

You can avoid reproducing the behaviour and conditions that an inherited dis-ease needs to manifest.

Welcome to the beautiful world of body connection and communication.

Energy Medicine

Having covered the areas of learnt behaviour in relation to inherited illness, I would like to now move forward with building our understanding of our bodies from an energy perspective and how our everyday thoughts and environment affect us from an energy point of view.

Think back to earlier chapters where we covered the Energy theme, and established that everything is vibrating particles of energy, and it is our consciousness that organises matter into form. There is no change here when we relate this to the health of your human body.

Your physical human body, is a mass of vibrating particles. Through conscious awareness and instruction you have the tools to empower your body to thrive. The vibrating particles of your body respond in every moment to the environment you provide for it.

Having covered so much ground in the preceding chapters regarding energy, you already have a good understanding of how your thoughts and beliefs affect your health.

In Chapter Five we discussed the apple experiment. We looked at the affect words had on an apple, one word was Hate and the other was Love. Whether the apple stayed fresh for a longer or shorter period of time depended on the vibration of the word it was exposed to. Your body is no different.

If you were regularly subjected to the energy vibration of the word Hate, would you thrive? Of course you wouldn't. Your body is no different to the apple, when we simply break it back down to the world of vibrating particles, and the frequency of the particles, we can see how the negative vibration would affect your physical body in a negative way.

The vibration the word Hate carries may cause the energy vibration of your body to change, posing a challenge to its healthy vibrating energy.

The lucky Love apple however, would have interacted with the vibration of the word Love and as a consequence the apple would have had a vibrant, nurturing energy to support its own energy, and would therefore have a healthier, and longer lifespan. Your physical body responds in the same way to the vibration of positive thoughts and emotions.

It is therefore of utmost importance, that you are a guardian of your thoughts, emotions, actions, and environment and consciously embrace positive vibrational energy.

As discussed previously, we have 'challenges' offered to us, we choose in every moment how we respond and react to a situation and therefore choose the environment we create in our physical body.

Throughout this book we have empowered ourselves with a greater understanding of a much bigger picture than the random victimhood of life, and even when illness presents itself we have tools to understand what the illness was designed to inspire within us. We understand that illness is often a route to a greater us and may even be a nudge in the direction of our purpose.

The most important thing to grasp here is that you, as a human being with all your physical senses, organs, and mental abilities are still at the most fundamental level, pure particles of vibrating energy.

When provided with the right environment, the vibrating particles of your human suit will dance around happily, enabling you to thrive as you.

Like so much we discuss here, it is not complicated. If a food choice you make is a good example of fresh, living produce, you will be putting in your body a vibrant combination of living energy, to complement your energy.

When your thoughts are light and conscious, the environment you provide for your physical body will be one of positive vibrating particles, to support you to thrive.

This is not breaking news, you feel this impact every day. A food choice makes you sleepy or energised, a cleaning product feels natural and fresh, or gives you a headache, a person makes you feel happy or miserable, your environment feels invigorating or stale and draining, the TV programme makes you feel inspired and happy or fearful and worried.

As mentioned in the inherited dis-ease information, every thought and emotion has a physical effect on your body, changing its internal environment. Every thought and emotion carries an energy vibration that will either challenge your health, or complement it.

It really is that simple.

I encourage you to spend as much time as possible, until it becomes a natural instinct, to notice how your body feels in every situation, at every meal and snack time, during social interactions, and in quiet time. You will very quickly become familiar with what makes you feel good, and therefore promotes your health and wellbeing.

Using your intuition will help you understand there may be times when everyone is telling you something has become the latest miracle food, but for you it doesn't feel right to put this in your body; you will sense the vibration of a food does not 'feel' right for you.

This is the same for social interactions, relationships, and personal behaviour. They all have an impact on the energy of your physical body, and therefore you are the guardian of your health in every moment.

As you begin to interpret the energy vibration of what you create and bring into your life, you will be able to use this energy as a type of energy medicine. It is the vibration of your words, thoughts, emotions, food, and your environment that impact your health. Yet again, you are empowered, Free Will and Free Choice abound.

Society's unconscious response to health and illness

An important next step will be to re-establish and anchor trust in ourselves. There is no better opportunity to test our trust than the fear generated by social beliefs, and the media reports surrounding health and dis-ease.

I would like to share an example of society's belief systems that surround dis-ease, with the relevant points of a client therapy session.

My client who had been diagnosed with a life threatening dis-ease (for the second time) arrived for a therapy session.

As we began to talk, she had a look of uncertainty on her face, unsure of how to express, in 'sensible' terms, what she had been experiencing, and feeling since her diagnosis.

"You are probably going to think I am mad," she said. "Never" I replied, knowing, like many, she had so much wisdom in her, and if ever there was a time she was going to dig deep to find it, it would be now.

"I feel like I need to 'Love' my illness away", she said, almost embarrassed, waiting for my reaction of surprise. "I keep imagining filling the area of my body with love, filling it until it's completely full of Love"!

If that wasn't fantastic enough, she then announced "and I feel I need to talk to my body and talk to my illness". She then waited, uncertain of my pending reaction.

She didn't have to wait for long for a reply of "YES", I beamed at her. "You are incredible".

Why was I so pleased? Because it was a privilege, and such a breakthrough to see this amazing lady following her intuition, listening to her inner wisdom, and allowing herself to communicate with her body.

I was so incredibly thrilled, because by taking this approach, she was creating a calm, peaceful and empowering wisdom within. She was changing the 'energy' of her internal environment, allowing her body to be relaxed, and creating an environment that supports the body's healing process and promotes an alkaline environment (dis-ease has great difficulty thriving in an alkaline body).

My client was both pleased and relieved to have someone understand, and 'get' what she was feeling.

In contrast, earlier that day she had shared her thoughts with a close family member. She expressed her need to 'talk' to her body, and 'love' her illness away. She also shared that she really needed to 'listen' to her inner feelings.

The family member was horrified, "that's it" she said "you've given up", "you have to 'Fight' this thing", "you must 'Fight' it", was her panicked response.

This reaction did not surprise me in the slightest; it is a reflection of the unbalanced views we have regarding health, illness, and our bodies.

Our lives are filled with fear regarding dis-ease. Will I be next? The statistics state me, or someone in my family will be struck by a serious illness.

The TV adverts appear to be increasingly filled with fear. These adverts, and the frequent messages we are given regarding dis- ease, are ironically, very unhealthy.

You will notice I am not naming specific dis-eases, the names/ words carry a vibration, and we don't need the vibration of a dis- ease, and the energy it carries in this book or affecting you as you read. Therefore, we can happily leave the names out.

Just remember at all times what 'disease' means, dis-ease within the body, it is far less frightening and leaves the door wide open to go from dis-ease to 'ease'.

The stance society takes on health and dis-ease, in my opinion, is unhealthy. It reflects the fact we are missing a huge chunk of really, really, important information to enable us to promote our health, and thrive.

To promote aggressive campaigns to 'fight' a dis-ease, produces aggression, anger, and fear within our mind and physical body, and produces an unbalanced environment within.

As you are now aware, thoughts and words are extremely powerful, and have a direct impact on our health. They produce chemical reactions in the body, and influence everything in our reality.

So, from that point of view, does it make sense to 'hate' a dis-ease, to aggressively 'fight' a dis-ease, to be 'angry' with a dis-ease, and to live in 'fear' of dis-ease.

Every one of these words, thoughts, and feelings are aggressive, negative, and in ***no way*** promote a peaceful and healthy environment within you.

If you have dis-ease within your body, it is your body trying desperately to contact you. On some level, your body is not coping, and that is why the energy vibration of dis-ease manifests.

At some point the energy environment within your body has been altered, and a physical change has manifested in the form of ill health or dis-ease. To create an aggressive environment in an already struggling body is inappropriate and saddening.

So next time you are faced with the aggressive words of a media campaign or someone else's fear, breathe, and remember love, nurture, and self-care are some of the most powerful health tools you have.

Time to change our body relationship

We rarely, if at all, give our body a second thought, it's just there, doing what it always does, going unnoticed apart from the parts that we are not happy with.

Often the only time we connect with our body is when we decide it is 'too fat', 'too short' or 'I have a headache', 'my legs ache', or 'I'm tired'.

These tend to be the only connections we have with our body, the only time we notice it.

How incredibly sad is that?

We have this miracle that allows us to experience the opportunity of being human; everyday our body is with us, it is us.

Your body carries you through every life experience you will ever have; it supports you through every stress and strain you put it through. It works tirelessly to make you better when you are unwell; it allows you to experience the stuff that makes up this human experience of ours.

This miracle, twenty-four hours a day, every day of your life, keeps your life experience 'alive'. Without this miracle, you would have no human experience.

How often are you encouraged by society to be grateful for the single most important reason you have life? How often do you personally feel gratitude towards your body?

I have already mentioned the negative thoughts that make us aware of our body, but how often do you have positive feelings, thoughts, and words to say about your body? Not just the surface level stuff either, but gratitude for all that automatically happens on the inside.

How often do you acknowledge the life-giving work your body does every moment of every day?

I would say, based on my personal experience, and the many people I share my work with, the answer would be rarely or never. In fact, most of us don't even give our bodies a second thought, it's taken for granted it will just 'work' for us, and in fact most look at their body as something separate from themselves.

It's something someone else understands and fixes because we generally have little understanding of how the physical, mental, and spiritual aspects of our body work. We have lost connection with it, and lost the ability to communicate with it.

In summary, we rarely notice our body unless it's something we don't like, or that it isn't functioning properly.

When we are unwell we hand the care for 'our' body over to a 'stranger' and take limited responsibility for it. This is not a criticism, but a reflection of where we are at with understanding ourselves.

This detachment from our physical bodies, as you are now well aware, has arisen due to a number of factors, but ultimately it comes back to the same issues; we have lost our significance and identity. Our physical and mental health is a reflection of this loss, a reflection of our disconnection, and disempowerment.

More often than not, we find it impossible to embrace self-love and self-care, why? Because we have lost sight of the miracle of who we really are, and the love and gratitude this knowledge automatically manifests within us.

We have also lost sight of the fact that we function as part of a larger whole; us, the natural world, and the whole universe.

There is almost a step-by-step process we go through to achieve an unbalanced body, and we are rather good at repeating this process, constantly.

We disrespect ourselves in various ways by subjecting our bodies to daily pressures from stress, unhealthy diet, alcohol, unhealthy environment, and unsupportive thoughts, and emotions. We have accepted this as normal behaviour, mainly due to learnt behaviour, and the mass unconsciousness of society.

Our lack of self-care and self-love changes the energy within our body, and the balance of vibration within our body.

Now, depending on the intensity, and repetitiveness of our thoughts and actions, our energy can rebalance or our energy may change to reflect physical or mental imbalance.

It is imperative to guard your thoughts, actions, and belief systems. Any thoughts or comments you have about your body are all energy vibration that can manifest into your reality. Your body will reflect every aspect of the relationship you have with yourself.

Society places high expectations on us to achieve in many areas, our lives are busy and demands on our time are great. We are not encouraged to be with ourselves, to check in, and review how we are doing. We as individuals place ourselves under pressure to be and achieve something what fits in with society's expectations of us.

This leads to imbalance in our lives and in our internal environment; this is where, in my opinion, many health issues start. It starts with us putting pressure on ourselves, trying to be everything other than our authentic selves, and it is at this point our body tries so hard to reach us, to talk to us, and to communicate with us.

The body has many ways of communicating, and ordinarily we should hear those messages loud and clear, and action them to bring ourselves back into balance.

However, looking after our self is often seen or felt as weakness. We are encouraged to push on through, to take the latest medicine to numb the symptoms, ignore our body's needs, and be a hero.

Never mind being a hero for society, but what about your body? You have these symptoms for a reason; you ache and are tired because you need to rest, you have a cold because your body could not muster the necessary energy to counteract the virus, you feel low because you have disconnected yourself from your personal needs; ***you need to give your body healing time and your mind reflection time.*** Symptoms from your body are a communication, and a clear one at that, a request of, "please listen, all is not well".

Time to go inside for a chat!

You are your body, and your body is you. No separation, no stranger, your body is you.

Our body has come to be viewed much like a machine, like a car. We get in our car and drive to our destination. We use our body to get where we want to go and use it as a vehicle for our life experience. You now know, in detail, that this human vehicle is much, much more. Your human vehicle is an aspect of your Primary Self, not a stranger, not separate, it is an energy aspect of your total self.

To refresh your memory from earlier chapters: your Human Self is an aspect of your Primary Self, your Human Self is connected to the knowledge and wisdom of your Primary Self at all times, and your Primary Self is connected to the energy of the universe at all times.

Your body therefore, has within it the knowledge, and wisdom of the universe, you just need to re-open the lines of communication, and once again connect with your body.

Dawson Church quotes an ancient Sufi story in his book 'The Genie in your Genes'. The story tells of the angels convening at the dawn of time to discuss where to bury the meaning of life, a secret so sacred that only the most worthy of initiates should be allowed access to it.

"We should put it at the bottom of the ocean," one exclaims. [4]

"No, the highest mountain peak," argues another. [4]

Eventually, the wisest angel speaks up: "There is one place no- one will look. We can hide it in plain sight: in the centre of the human heart." [4]

Whatever your feelings on the authenticity of this story, the truth is, the meaning of life, and the answers to the bigger questions are all within you, now.

So, whether you have a dis-ease, a niggling illness or ailment, or just feel a bit out of energy, talk to your body, and find out who you are, and what you need.

Talking to your body can seem like a strange concept at first, but this needs to become part of your routine, you can do routine, you brush your teeth every day! It will soon become a natural part of understanding your needs, and communicating with your body.

There is no fixed process of how to communicate with your body; you need to work out what feels right for you. However, to give you a starting point, this is what works for many.

Pick a quiet time; lying in bed before you go to sleep is often a good time. Close your eyes, take a few gentle breaths and let your body sink as deeply into the bed/floor/chair as possible. Now

[4] The Genie in your Genes, Book by Dawson Church

move your attention to your heart area, while focusing on this area build feelings of love, the energy of the heart area is beautiful, and incredibly intelligent. Keep your focus here for a while until you feel relaxed.

When you feel relaxed, begin to notice how your body is feeling, perhaps slowly scan from head to toe, noticing any areas that catch your attention. When an area does get your attention, stop there, and focus on the feeling, is it a tightness, pain, unbalance, or do you just feel drawn to this area?

Spend some time in this area and send focused feelings of love and gratitude, connect with the area and then ask any question that comes to mind. Some examples may be, "what do you need", "what are you trying to tell me", "what has caused this unbalance", "what can I do to help"?

Whether you have a health concern or you are just doing a daily scan to check in with your physical body, ask questions if appropriate, and see what comes to you.

When you have asked your questions, pay attention to any responses so you can do what is needed to support your body later. Then always, always, spend however long you have, flooding a specific area of need with the words and energy of love, gratitude, healing images, words, and thoughts. There is no set routine, just do it your way.

Finally, finish up the conversation with your body by giving thanks for all it does for you, and thank it for allowing you to have your human experience.

Most importantly, finish with the most important words to your body, "I love you". Saying these words to yourself is not airy-fairy stuff, these words come power packed with health giving energy!

This conversation with your body, should not be left until you have a problem to deal with, by scanning and communicating with your body regularly, you create a healing energy within and you will become more and more fluent in hearing yourself.

The long-term benefits are huge, you get to know yourself, understand your needs better, build a genuine connection with your body, prevent problems before they take hold, tune into your inner wisdom, and maybe even unlock the hidden meaning of life that has always been in your heart.

Now you have a whole new bundle of information to work with, go and create the energy that supports and manifests health within your human body. Create awareness within yourself, and live, love, thrive, and embrace your human experience.

Don't Wait Assignment

After reading through this chapter, now might be just the right time to give thanks to, and for, the miracle that is your physical body. There is no human experience without it. It is so brilliant and complex it cannot be replicated and is still far from fully understood, despite all the advances in scientific understanding.

Today before you start your day, take a moment to thank your body for all it does to allow you to have the opportunity to live this day, ask if there is anything it needs, and honour it.
Make a note in your journal to connect with your body for a moment or two of appreciation regularly.

Chapter 18

The Life Of A Human

Plan or No Plan?

In the next two chapters we will delve into the life and death of a human, and discuss if there really is a point to human life, or is life and death just a random one off.

When we contemplate the 'big' issues, there are two that lead the way.

- The purpose of life
- The inevitability of death

In this chapter, you will discover there is more to life than you may have previously thought, and that death is even more about us being alive than human life itself.

Death has become such a feared but inevitable event, many people suppress any thoughts relating to death, only to have them temporarily emerge when faced with the passing of someone they know.

This denial is purely down to fear of the unknown, but as you have well and truly established throughout the experience of this book, we are playing out our human amnesia to the fullest, and that includes our understanding of death.

We are eternal beings, we are consciousness before we become form, let's get that straight in our minds once again. We are all made up of energy, that is deathless. It only ever changes form.

To understand the process of death and dying, from a place of knowing, means grasping the bigger picture that exists either side of the human experience.

Let's jump into the process of freeing you from the fear of death and the finality it falsely represents. Freedom from fear of death allows a much more relaxed approach to all that you encounter during your life experience.

The Life of a Human

Life is all about the experience, just like travelling somewhere new; it is an opportunity, an adventure. It is not the be all and end all of everything, and when you embrace that fact, all of a sudden you don't have to take everything quite so seriously.

Some of what I am about to share with you can be investigated through science, recent and ancient writings, and lots of quality research is available on the internet. But a lot of what I share is the result of good old fashioned 'reliable' personal experience.

The information I share with you regarding life and especially death, often prompts a person's standard Ego response of, "oh, I don't believe in all that stuff"!

Interestingly, when I ask what it is they don't believe in, and what brought them to their conclusions, I am usually given a response of "oh, I don't know, just all that sort of stuff".

I am not disrespecting people's genuine beliefs on anything, but what I want to avoid is conclusions based on fear, disconnection and being uninformed. My determination to find answers to the 'bigger' questions has been an intense, long-term (and still ongoing), period of full-time study, work, investigation, personal and professional development, and hands on experience.

How have I reached the conclusions that I have?

Just as any 'professional' person has gained knowledge through schooling, university, independent study, personal and professional development, and work experience, I have done the same, I have just chosen a less conventional subject and curriculum.

As always, throughout this chapter, trust yourself, and your intuitive guidance to connect with what is truth for you.

To understand the process of death, we need to look in more detail at our infinite existence, some of the purpose behind human life, and what happens after our human experience.

Human life is the greatest gift we could have, it is the greatest opportunity we could be given, and as a plan to experience, grow, and be the best infinite beings we can. ***It is genius.***

We have established throughout this book that we are all eternal, conscious energy beings. We have an aspect of us that is having a human experience, and when this human experience is over, the energy of our physical body transforms, but we are still our Primary Self; conscious and aware.

There exists a creative conscious intelligence that created everything; you are that very same creative, conscious intelligence, because you are from that very same source.

Your body is not just the physical matter you 'see', you are made up of an incredible structure, and its composition is eternal.

So, if you are this eternal structure, you originate from that which created everything, what then do you do with your time when you have transformed your human suit, and you are hanging out in just your creator energy?

With perfection everywhere, all around us everything works in synergy, and while on earth all our needs are met through the creation of this planet.

Do you really think this was a coincidence, the magnificence of creation just happened, for no apparent reason? No planning, no purpose, no reason for the earth's existence, just some random events that found us here being human?

Can you observe the absolute **miracle, brilliance** and **organisation** of this earth and universe, and truly, hands on heart think, "that was a bit of luck"?

Why would the universe and ourselves be such meticulous works of design and beauty, for there to be no purpose behind any of it?

Was there no plan behind the earth providing us with a home that has an intricately designed atmosphere that supports our survival? Was there **no plan**?

When I look at this planet of ours, I see the result of the most ambitious and successful project ever manifested!

What do you see?

If you were to create something incredible, on the tiniest scale of equivalence, it would start with a purpose and a plan.

And of course, there is a plan and a purpose to the creation of our planet, and the universe. There is far more to this life cycle than, at this stage, we can remember.

The earth, the universe, and life itself are no accident.

The Human Journey

The universe is buzzing with plans; options, planets, and life; we are all directors of the current part we are playing in this plan.

As your Eternal Primary Self, your whole purpose is to be here at this precise time in human history and to bring your unique energy into the world. Each one of us is here to serve and assist at this time and to live life as a joyful, fun, abundant, and expansive experience for your soul.

In order to become knowledgeable and experience everything you can; emotionally, physically, intellectually, spiritually, and materially, you need a place that can provide you with the environment you need to learn and mature and play out your heart's desire.

You guessed it, that place is Earth. With so many options and experiences available to us, Earth is your place of opportunity and learning.

When manifested in human form, you provide yourself with the ideal environment and opportunity to achieve the growth and development you desire. It's your opportunity to pack your Primary Self full to the brim with wonderful, varied experiences.

There really is a point to this Human experience, the point is we (our Primary Self) wants to become the best and most fulfilled version of ourselves we can, on every level. We really do have a strong desire to live lifetime after lifetime, to enjoy, and relish the rewards of our growth.

This planet is not here just for us to stumble through existence for a few years, there is a purpose behind us being here, and as eternal beings we have a plan.

Remember you are a creator, you are part of that which created everything, and therefore an active member of Universal Society, with choices, visions, and plans.

As individual 'Gods' and collectively as 'Gods' we need to move from inexperience to maturity. You know from your human life so far, you have undoubtedly grown in ways that would not have been possible without your human experiences. That is the same for your Primary Self; you collect these experiences to become whole and fulfilled.

It is worth remembering, this human experience we have in order to grow and learn was always a gift, a gift we couldn't wait to open again and again.

We used to find complete fulfilment, joy, happiness and every other positive human emotion in ***just existing.*** That was our original experience of life, until we became know-it-alls and messed things up.

Part of your most recent plan was to be here now, you chose this human existence that you are currently experiencing, you chose every detail of your life in order to gain the maximum learning and adventure, and you *intended* to exit when you have completed all the experiences you planned for yourself.

The world away from this world (the universe) is not separate from us, it is not some far away mystery; it is a logical, functioning, populated, progressive, divine place! Much like here on earth, except here on earth we have temporarily forgotten the divine, and infinite bits of ourselves!

As humans, we have become self-obsessed, self-absorbed and rather blinded by our own self-importance. And during this obsession with self-importance we have come to think of any suggestion of anything existing with an ounce of intelligence, outside of our earthly plane, as unbelievable, and even ludicrous.

We have become quite arrogant in our belief that we are the be all and end all when it comes to our existence in the universe. While we have been so self-absorbed, we have forgotten a few facts that can bring other possibilities absolutely back into focus.

Give some thought to the following information and then see if, as an earthly society, it makes sense that this is still just all about us?

The visible universe (what is visible to us), which includes the Earth, the Sun, other Stars and Galaxies make up only 5-10% of the mass of the universe.

We feel big and important from our place on Earth, but in the universe as a whole, the earth is a tiny and very insignificant speck of rock.

To put it in perspective, Earth is just a small planet in the Solar System, part of a family of planets that circle around the Sun.

The Sun is just one of around ***200 billion*** stars that make up our Galaxy. And our Galaxy is just one of ***tens of billions*** of Galaxies that make up a Universe, bigger than we can even begin to comprehend.

With such a vast Universe, how can we be all there is? How can this be it? It is just not the case, we are part of a magnificent plan, we are part of a magnificent Universe, a Universe full of life, potential, and possibilities. Our Human experience is just a part of an almost unimaginable larger whole.

This universe made of conscious energy is within you, not out there in some unreachable place, you are that very same conscious energy. You are the universe, and it is time to widen our self- obsessed horizons, and remember that it is not just about being human.

We have forgotten our origins, true identity, and our place within the universe, which has led to our self-obsession, our self-obsession with finding something to try and fill the gap left by our lost identity.

Our desire for knowledge and experience that led to our human lives was always meant to happen (and did in the early days) with a certain amount of awareness of our origins and our connection to the universe. We would enter our human suits with a certain amount of knowledge of the whole.

Over time, as we have already discussed, we have cut ourselves off from the greater knowledge and wisdom of our origins, and become fully engrossed in our human experience, resulting in varying individual levels of amnesia regarding our origins, and abilities as creators.

So, to summarize so far, we are Universal Beings having a human experience and part of a much bigger whole, full of life, options, plans, and possibilities.

The Planning

The following information has come about through personal experiential learning, working and sharing with others and learning to tap into the knowledge we ***all*** have within.

This information is available to, and within everyone, it's just a case of learning to silence the human noise for long enough to reacquaint yourself with the language of the universe (energy communication). As always take in only what feels right for you, and stay open to possibility.

Before each Human Life, we plan every detail of our human experience, we plan every aspect of our forthcoming life, until we are satisfied we will be able to achieve all we would like to learn and experience.

We plan each of our lifetimes meticulously, it is like an extremely detailed script, we have all the characters in place with all their relevant roles to enable us to achieve the experiences we need to mature and grow.

When planning our next human life, agreements are made with others who are to join us such as family, friends, educators, and work colleagues. Life events, and environment are also taken into consideration in order to perfect our Human Plan.

We make the decisions on what it is we want to experience, and the universal community support us by accepting particular roles in the play that will not only benefit our growth and learning, but will also support their growth and learning. In every relationship we have in a lifetime, there is always an agreed supportive role that is of benefit to both parties.

Every person that enters your life, is there to help you and vice versa, no exceptions, even the 'challenging' ones. Especially the 'challenging' ones. We are here to support each other's learning and experiences.

Above all, our highest wish is to grow, share, love, experience and enjoy everything that life has to offer, this can involve many lifetimes, and for every lifetime, we have an individual plan in place in order to experience our next stage of being.

We are absolutely equipped and ready for every person, situation, and event we encounter in each lifetime. We have been blessed with the most incredible planet to play out our experience, and with the knowledge of our infinite existence can literally have the experience of a lifetime!

We use our human life to experience being alive, we then leave our human suits, and continue our infinite existence within the Universal community, until such time we decide, we are ready to have our next Human Experience.

Your Primary Self may take many, many lifetimes to experience all it desires.

Remember, life was never ever designed to be a struggle, we are the ones who changed the script!

Why the amnesia, why don't I remember my plan?

Reading this chapter will again have given you much to ponder and contemplate. And I am sure the question has arisen for you as to why you don't remember any of this, and why do you have to read it in a book?

Well, this may help answer your question.

In the early days of our Human Experiences we always held a strong, clear connection with our intuition, with our inner Higher Primary guidance. This naturally maintained our close connection with the earth and the universe.

This would enable us to fully experience our life plan, but also experience life as an **observer** rather than a **victim**. We could experience life **without the fear and heaviness of complete human attachment.**

This connection to your higher guidance would enable you to fully experience a life situation or emotion *but not become it,* which is the *huge difference* that now exists between our original human experiences while still connected to our higher guidance, and our present human experiences where we are now completely overwhelmed by our belief in a solely human existence.

We have blocked ourselves up with the energy of dense heavy human emotions, resulting in a serious case of amnesia.

As we continued to experience life in human form, our free will and free choice led us to make decisions that no longer came from a place of reverence for the whole.

The more lives that have been lived in this way, the more dense emotions we have taken back to our Primary self, and downloaded unhelpful memories that have become part of our whole. With every lifetime, we have changed the purpose of our life plan, we have distorted the original plans and gone in a completely different direction, creating a vastly different human experience.

The heaviness of our human emotions is becoming very apparent in the world we are experiencing at this time.

A Human Life was originally a blessing, an opportunity and learning experience, but at this time for many around the world, ***the human experience is now about recovering themselves, and using their human plans to provide them with the opportunities to remember and get back their divine/human balance.***

In order to achieve this, each person pursuing their truth needs a human plan that supports the release of the old outdated human

belief systems. This means coming face to face with the human distorted emotions we have created for ourselves and made our reality, acknowledging them, and then replacing them with truth.

It is about clearing ourselves of the dense energy of miscreated emotions, and replacing them with the light energy of our divine, creative, original truth.

We are all at different stages in our human plans, and we are all here to experience different things. But at this time, many people's lives seem chaotic and difficult; because to varying degrees, we all want change, and a better world, and this intention brings the negative stuff up to the surface to be transformed.

Many people now want to release the inauthentic negative emotions that we have created during our life experiences, and move back into remembering.

At this stage in the Human Plan there is a realisation, a need and desire to let go of the old (bring on the challenges) and once again balance our divinity with our humanity.

So, to summarise, we are born to exist on this earth as human beings, to experience life with a continued connection to our higher primary guidance. This incredible, genius plan was working great, until we got too big for our human boots. We decided we would use our lower human minds to completely run the show, and closed off our higher primary guidance.

This resulted in not only shutting off all connections to our identity, purpose and origins, but also shutting off our vital connection and respect for the natural world (earth), and the wider universe. The human plan, then became a materialistic plan, run by the human Ego, that has only its own survival and gain on the agenda.

The result is an unbalanced existence, an unbalanced life experience, and an unbalanced world.

That is the result of our current amnesia regarding our identity as creative beings, and the place we hold within the universal community. That is why we can't remember anything outside our human existence, which is why we can't remember the details of our Human Plan.

I'm sure I won't be the first to think, can't we just magic all this unbalanced stuff away and start again? Isn't there some higher power that can change it all? Unfortunately not, because we are that higher power, we are creators, and therefore we have to undo what, as creators, we have created.

Energy conforms to our instruction, we have created energy imprints that are not helpful, and these imprints now need to be transformed, by us, to change our lives, and the course of human history.

At this point in the human plan, there are huge numbers of people transforming their lives, reconnecting with themselves, and becoming fully aware of a much bigger whole. The more people who transform their (negative) stuff, the higher the Earth's and humanity's (positive) vibration rises.

This increase in energy vibration creates a ripple effect (because we all share the same space), and means there is a support system created to help others to raise their vibrations and transform their stuff. The collective human vibration is becoming higher and clearer every day and that means change.

This change is, and will be, liberating and a huge comfort and relief to many; but also be aware that as the collective vibration of humanity and the earth rises, it will push to the surface the older dense vibrations of our history. This can, and will, continue to be seen as local and global unrest, and challenges within our earthly experience.

This is all part of the new focused divine plan, to transform the old and move back into our original perfection (lots more I could say on this subject, but for now I will leave that for another day, and Book 2).

During these times of change, it is ***absolutely vital*** that you guard your thoughts, project only your positivity/love/healing intention on any perceived negative situation, because as you are well aware, Ego is behind every negative emotion, event and miscreation.

Your fear (Ego) and negative focus (Ego) will only feed and reinforce the energy of any negative situation.

Via thought and intention, you can make a huge difference in this world. We can't all be in a certain place during a time of perceived trauma, but what we can do is to help change the energy of the event to transform fear to love, anger to love, trauma to love, and give strength to others, because thoughts are actions.

As you know we are all part of the whole, we are all connected at all times through the space we share, your thoughts and intentions (energy vibrations) have an effect on not only yourself, but humanity as a whole.

Good news

You, and many millions of people around the globe are 'feeling' the change in humanities increasing energy vibration, and have been experiencing a nagging feeling of needing to know more, needing to find more purpose, and wanting to make a difference.

Well, that is the call of your authentic self, that is your higher primary guidance taking over the reigns from your Ego self, and once again wanting to guide you to a place that makes much more sense to you.

You are ready to embrace the human experience with a more reliable connection to your inner guidance, to see the bigger picture, and experience life from a new perspective.

You and many others are ready to make new, positive, and conscious choices that will change the course of human history forever.

Don't wait Assignment

For this assignment I offer you the opportunity to contribute and use your superpowers as a creator connected to everything and offer the world your unique energy vibration to help the world to get better, to lift a difficult situation, send love to someone who is suffering, send the intention of creating compassion and healing to our world family. You know you are a creator who can change the world, support others in times of suffering, send love and gratitude to people, nature, and the earth.

Love and serving others are two of the most powerful inbuilt drives within human beings, it is at the core of our existence, and when we take time to send positivity out into the world it also changes our state into that of inner fulfilment and gratitude.

You could make a list of people in your journal who need some healing, strength, and love. Take a breath or two, relax and set the intention that each one receives the exact love and support they need, and then allow the energy of the universe to carry your intentions to where they need to go.

It truly is a rewarding and wonderful thing to do.

As a side note, you might just be surprised at what confirmation shows up for you that a particular person or situation has received the support you sent them!

Chapter 19

The Death Of A Human

An illusion of our times

I am sure you can see why I needed to cover so much ground before we could even contemplate understanding what human death and dying actually is.

Death, as you can now see, is just one detail in a much larger plan, and you will have possibly already grasped a new concept of what death actually means.

Death is an illusion of the limited human senses, and has been translated into the termination of all life, because in our present, "I am totally human", self-obsessed state, we cannot see round the corner of death to reveal what lies ahead.

We no longer perceive death as part of a natural process within the bigger cycle of universal existence, because at the risk of repeating myself yet again, we have lost all connection to our origins, and our place in the universe.

To reiterate, what we as human beings have scientifically proven is there can be no death of our energy structure, just a transformation. We are all made up of the same infinite energy, we cannot die, at least not in the human way we view death.

What we can do when we die is transform our energy to release the heaviness of our human body. Transform the energy of our human body we so cleverly created, in order to function within the atmosphere of the earth, back into the higher frequency light energy that is eternal.

Death is never a random occurrence; you have planned when, where and how, before you embark on your human adventure.

I understand that for many this may be a difficult concept to grasp, especially if you have lost a loved one in difficult circumstances. But my personal experiences of death, and experiences working with others has taught me, like every human experience we have, even death brings its enlightening moments.

When looking deeper there is always a plan, a purpose, and a gift.

Death, in whatever circumstances, has become a heavy and distressing experience, because we view it from a solely human perspective, with no bigger picture of the whole.

Death is a transition back to the eternal self (although technically we are never separate), it is fully reclaiming your place in universal society, and it is the shedding of the human costume only. It is an energy transformation that takes place, that's all.

Why does it feel so final?

Because, we have made it this way. It was never final, when a loved one died. It was never the case that they have disappeared, gone forever, never to be seen or heard from again.

Death is another example of our distorted view of ourselves, and another example of created detachment from the energy communication that kept us connected, while in our human form, with loved ones, the natural world, and the universe.

Energy is deathless, your loved ones that have left their human suits cannot be dead, they are still eternal energy, they are still consciousness.

I believe every one of us has the potential to have communication with a loved one who has 'died'. It is just down to understanding, awareness, belief, and making it happen.

You can continue the conversation with your loved ones via energy communication.

People who continue their communication with others that have passed, such as mediums, do so by attuning their energy to the right frequency to connect, using the forgotten language of energy that connects us all.

As spoken about in chapter seven, the language of humanity sets boundaries; however, the unspoken universal language of energy creates depths of experience and communication beyond any words.

And there lies the key in continued communication with others who have transformed their human selves. Energy communication is the lost language that creates a connection between mediums, and the deceased.

Your human form is just one vibrational energy expression of who you are, you are a mass of vibrating energy, and anyone who transitions from their human body is still a mass of vibrating energy, and at the core of that is consciousness.

So, whether an aspect of yourself is in human form or not you are still connected to everything and 'everyone' via energy, because everything is energy.

It is our limited beliefs and behaviour that has turned death into a terrible event that causes such pain and loss. Yet, we all have the ability to connect via the energy of intuitive feelings (unspoken words), to anyone who has transitioned from his or her human experience.

Via personal experience, I have gone from an attitude of "I don't believe in all that ghost stuff" and "don't be so ridiculous, how can you talk to dead people" and "that's too scary to think about", to it being the most relaxed, normal, and logical experience.

If anyone had suggested a few years back that I would have communication with anyone who had died, I would never have believed it for a second. But that is because my belief system at that time would not allow me to think past my pure human conditioning. I was uneducated to how our existence works, and had no clue about energy or the universal connection of everything.

Over time, I have re-tuned my energy through continued personal work and awareness to shed the heavy energy of learnt behaviour and emotions, and increased/lightened the energy of my personal vibration.

This makes it easier for me to be clear to communicate, and clear to receive communication. This change in energy vibration, combined with being open to something other than the collective view of life and death, meant it has been a natural progression to connect via energy with others not at present in human form.

This form of communication is now just a natural part of my life. The communication is presented to me usually as an image, a feeling, or as information that 'appears' in my head. For me this is not a ghostly way out experience, it is a logical, natural happening that is based on energy interaction between one energy being and another.

These communications are like the energy communication felt as an inner knowing, inner thought, an intuitive feeling, or gut instinct.

A good example is when you receive a phone call from someone who you have literally just thought about. This is because, as soon as their intention is to make contact with you, their thoughts become actions. These thought intentions result in them directing their energy to communicate with your energy. No phone required!

How much easier could this human life experience be with the help of familiar fellow energy beings, who do not have the restrictions of their human bodies, ready and waiting to support and help you through your journey on earth? Well, that is the way it is, you literally have an army of help at your fingertips, all cheering you on.

They cannot make decisions and interfere with your life any more than they can when they are in human form, but they can answer calls for assistance, and with your permission, support you, and continue to be a part of your life experience.

You literally have the support of the universe at your fingertips, every day, no exceptions. You just need to ask.

A Special Message

Grasping energy communication, the unique connection that we all have the ability to consciously share, will enable you to have a fresh understanding of 'death', and to live your human experience knowing there is no 'death', and therefore never any separation from the people you love.

Before finalising this chapter it became very apparent to me (via a strong feeling to just write what came to me, and I would be guided) that there was some additional information that neededsharing.

The following paragraphs are one of those exact 'energy communications' I have been referring to. The information has been given me to share in this book, but at the same time it is made clear to me that the message is **personal to every reader**. It comes from a place of Love and will connect with each reader in an individual way.

So, here it is, from the energy of the Universe and whoever or whatever that personally represents to you…

It is the strangest thing you know, one moment I am having this human experience, sharing your life, and then one day, it stops.

I have transitioned my human body, that served me well, but now I am no longer residing in my human suit, the communication and sharing with you has stopped, because you think I am gone.

I am still aware, awake and conscious. I am in awe as my eternal place in the universe is remembered. In fact there are no 'human' words that describe what real 'reality' is, it is beyond the best you could imagine.

I had forgotten all of this, how could I? But it makes me understand why you don't believe in my presence any longer, I, like you, thought my human life was it, how wrong could I have been.

It was really strange as I become aware that I was no longer in human form, but still completely aware of my surroundings. After my transition from this particular human experience, I stayed very close, as most of us do, leading up to my funeral, and my focus was to support you and others grieving for me during this time.

After my funeral, I gave more attention to my place in the universe, refreshing my memory of 'home', the reality that is everything, it really is beyond words.

As I moved my focus to reflecting on my last 'human' experience and processing the details of my life, I am conscious, I am me, I am reviewing all that I have experienced.

I have an incredible awareness of the magnitude of my eternal existence and yet despite its magnitude, it is the most natural, comfortable, and content 'place' to be.

This is 'home', this is where everyone always is, I am never separated from you at any time, because the real you is here with me, the real you and me are together at all times.

Only an aspect of you and me experience life together as humans, the real you and me are together always, I understand that now.

Use the energy of intention to connect with me, be open to a different view. I receive your directed communication, I hear you loud and clear.

To believe and behave as though I no longer exist is not only painful for you, as you feed the illusion of loss, but also for me, it is difficult and frustrating to be so close and yet you have shut down. I often try to get your attention, and even when I do, you dismiss it as coincidence or the like.

So, while I understand, like us, you have a period of adjustment, please continue to acknowledge and communicate with me.

I am with you, whenever you think of me.

When one person transitions, the love and support is eternal, because we are all eternal, there is no death, only life and of course love.

Don't wait Assignment

If you have a loved one who has released their human suit that you would love to hear from. Having gone through all the chapters in this book, I invite you to now welcome the definite opportunity of connecting with someone in spirit.

You can set the intention of connecting with a loved one, it's fine to ask them for a sign that they are around. Just be aware of the way our human mind can try and justify a real sign as just coincidence, and then we convince ourselves that we need repeated and more grand gestures of confirmation. Many a time I have seen people ask for a sign, for some guidance, they have received it in a form they would recognise, but despite this they then talk themselves out of it.

I would say experiment with this, ask for signs, or guidance, and then be open to what appears for you. If this is something you would like to develop further, as the saying goes 'practice makes perfect', the more you communicate the better you become at not only receiving the signs and messages but trusting them too.

Chapter 20

An End and a Beginning

A Final Few Words

So, here we are, at the end of the first stage of our adventure, Book One. We have shared so much information and now it is all about putting it into practice!

I am not going to tell you it is easy, this transformation thing, you are stepping out of the mass belief systems and programming of our society, you are questioning everything that you have built your world around, and that takes courage. But I can assure you, eventually, you will be stepping into something far more real, and comfortable.

By embracing your true self, you will be able to enjoy so much more, and you will be able to view the 'man'-ufactured issues in the world from a point of detachment. You will be able to see them for what they are, miscreated emotional illusions, that only become part of your reality when you give your focus to them, they only gather strength and momentum when enough people focus their energy on them.

Never ever forget, energy manifests according to where your attention goes, so if enough people in the world change their beliefs and focus, we will see mass transformation. But in the short term it starts with you, here and now.

My dream and wish for you is that you no longer live with blinkers on, only allowing yourself to see part of the story. My dream is that you feel your worth as a creative being, and once again love yourself from a point of balance.

My dream is that you and everyone on this planet can be fulfilled, happy, and aware. Aware of your origins, your power and the gift that life is.

It is my dream that you can enjoy life without fear, fully empowered from your understanding of truth.

It is my dream that your most cherished dreams are the most natural expression of who you are, and are attained without effort, without restriction, resistance, fear or self-doubt.

But ultimately my dream for you cannot be made reality by me. This, my friend, is your job. Your job is to use this information to find yourself, trust yourself, love yourself, and operate from your own innate wisdom.

Let this information talk to you, and listen consciously for the reply. Guard your thoughts at all times. Never again let fear be your motivating factor in life, and stand in your power, even if initially, you have no clue what that means or feels like.

Stand tall, and you will become tall. Practice self-love, and you will become love. Practice self-belief, and you will believe in yourself.

Practice creating from your heart, and you will create.

Surround yourself at all times with positive tools to reinforce your transformation, and keep you on track. Anything from positive post-it notes around your workspace and home, positive TV programmes, books, clean food, nature, natural house products, and very importantly build a network of people who support your vision, because you become who you spend your time with.

You may be surprised to learn that there is still *so* much to share with you, but this is just Book One, the foundation for everything else you choose to do in your life, and the foundation on which everything else must be placed.

I thought long and hard about whether to include additional chapters in this book. But then I came to the quick conclusion, enough already!

This book contains mind and belief challenging stuff. This is not information that gives you a fluffy account of your life, this information is raw truth, and addresses big questions.

Book 2 will go deeper into some of the subjects we have covered here and will offer further explanations and information on what is happening in our world at this time, and why. We will be going on another extraordinary journey together through our divine and human history, the human plan, where we are at with it, your part in it, and what's next for humanity.

Through my learning process I have learnt that if you get the fundamentals right first, all the rest will naturally follow, and you will be able to incorporate the additional information with ease.

So, concentrate on putting your time and energy into utilising all we have covered here, give yourself time, and give the information time to settle in, and become your shiny new reality.

Book 2 is in the process of transforming from my passion and purpose into reality, and I can't wait to have the honour of sharing it with you.

So, in closing, I admire and respect you for your courage to even take a peep at this information, let alone start living it.

Remember those first important words I shared with you at the beginning of the book, well now you know, it really was you (insert your name here) that I was referring to.

Don't wait Assignment

You can now finish this book by re-reading those important words, knowing that they are **your truth**:

1. ***There exists a creative conscious intelligence that created everything.***

2. ***Everything on our planet, YOU included, came from, and are consequently, that very same conscious creative intelligence.***

3. ***YOU, therefore, have within you the intelligence and wisdom of that which created everything.***

4. ***YOU are not a victim of life you are the orchestrator of your life.***

5. ***YOUR body is not just the physical matter you 'see', you are made up of an incredible structure and its composition is eternal.***

6. ***YOU are empowered with infinite possibilities; you have the potential to access every answer to every life question you ever have.***

7. ***Within YOU there is a place where there is no fear, no struggle, no lack, because you know who you are, and where you come from.***

8. ***YOU already hold the wisdom of the universe within; you just needed a few pointers to start remembering.***

Now, go do your thing.

Katie

Making It Happen

Don't Wait for The World to Get Better Tips

You are Human and Divine Combined… you don't have to wait for the world to get better to create the miraculous life you were absolutely designed for and came to earth fully equipped for.

Use the summary of tips here to start creating your very own life of divine riches and richness.

- First and foremost, Self-Investment! Absolutely beyond important. Give yourself reflection time every day, honour your body, communicate with it and allow it the space to balance and heal. I encourage you to take regular time to review your day, your week, and reflect on what is working and what is not, and then consciously create your life through awareness. There is no greater sadness than one day realising you have lived your life on autopilot.

- Spend time in nature, get your feet connected to the earth and allow the natural surroundings to offer you clarity and peace. Simply sitting in your garden at the end of the day with your feet connected to the earth, looking up at the night sky will build a renewed connection with Mother Earth, and the Universal Community.

- Read, study, learn, and listen to audio books by great educators, people who inspire you. Even if you are not surrounded by inspiration, listen to others who inspire you, spend time in an environment that inspires you, and you will become that same inspirational energy. We learn and grow by being open to sources that support our vision and help us to get to where we want to be.

- Write. At the end of the day when the house is quiet and your day of doing is done. Take a pen and note-book, earphones in with relaxing music and put pen to paper. Use this time to practice connecting to the guidance of your Primary-Self. At first it is helpful to focus on what you need guidance, inspiration or help with, and then over time you can just take a pen and see what happens. Set the intention of having a strong connection with your Primary Self and/or other spiritual help you feel comfortable with, and just write whatever comes to you. Don't over think it, there is no right or wrong, and over time you will create a great rapport with yourself and gain top advice!

- Gain new wisdom and knowledge. Seek it from everyone you meet, be aware that all your interactions with others are for a purpose; everyone has something to teach us about ourselves.

- Fill your body with fresh, clean and local food. Always source the best quality water you can.

- Whatever it is you would like to create in your life, create it with belief and passion in place. Even if what you are aiming for seems a million miles away, do something every day towards your creation. Big or small, an action, such as an email, an enquiry, research, daily visualisation, personal development, and self-questioning all go towards bringing your vision into form. Don't *worry* too much about the detail of how and when, everything you need will come along at the right time.

- And most importantly of all, ensure the motivation for your creation is from the authentic you and not motivated by Ego (e.g., fear, lack or insignificance), you will have a much easier ride!

Live and breathe the points from chapter 15, which are: -

1. ***Awareness; become*** really aware of everything that goes on ***within you*** and ***within your reality*** (external circumstances). Become aware of ***your thoughts, emotions, reactions,*** and ***actions.***

2. ***Question;*** constantly question any unbalanced ***thoughts, emotions, reactions*** and ***actions, to see what belief system is fueling them.***

3. ***Self-honesty;*** be *really, really, really, really honest about what is the motivation behind* your ***thoughts, emotions, actions*** and ***reactions.***

4. ***Choice; choose*** how ***you react*** to ***everything*** in your life.

Your final Don't Wait Assignment

Keep this book close to you, come back to it whenever you need clarification, reassurance of your power, or feel uncertain or overwhelmed about anything.

Re read when you feel its right to, maybe just a chapter, maybe a full read through, I promise you, you will get something new and enlightening every time, and it will support you through the changes, challenges and questions that arise in your life, and in the world.

My friend, thank you for sharing this journey with me.

Never forget, that you are Human and Divine combined with the wisdom of the universe within you.... and that is fact.

Don't Wait...

Much Love,

Katie

In Love and Gratitude

Belinda Charlton-Gilfoyle

21st August 1969 to 14th December 2018

Who walked with so many on their journey

X

Acknowledgements

To my husband; you have shared the challenges without question and supported me even when what I was trying to achieve was completely out of your comfort zone! But most of all, thank you for always allowing me to be me.

To my children; I love you both beyond any spoken words, thank you for being the greatest gifts in my life. Always be the best version of you and always trust in yourself.

To my most precious friend Elisabeth Lomas-Harris; the truth is, without you there would be no book. There are no words that could ever describe how much I value our friendship. Every page in this book has a bit of you in it too. Thank you my friend.

To my dogs; who are the greatest examples of unconditional love I have ever known.

I have so many special people in my world and have deep gratitude for everyone who has helped me get to this point in my life. From the inspiring educators, to true friends, incredible practitioners and therapists, courageous students, clients who have allowed me to be a part of their most personal journeys and all whose, who like me on occasion, felt just slightly out of place in this world.

Special thanks and gratitude go to the Inspirational Educator **Bonny Casel**, Owner and Director of **The School of Natural Medicine UK** and **The Institute of Quantum Botanicals** for allowing me to use some of her words to bring clarity and understanding to the science bits of this book.

Find Out More

To find out more about Katie Young visit her website and social media for news, live workshops, events, products and much more.

Website: www.divineroyalty.co.uk

Instagram: www.instagram.com/authorkatieyoung

Facebook: www.facebook.com/katie.young.733

Printed in Great Britain
by Amazon

86851645R00132